THE RETURN OF THE VANISHING AMERICAN

BY LESLIE A. FIEDLER

NONFICTION

An End to Innocence
No! in Thunder
Love and Death in the American Novel
Waiting for the End
The Return of the Vanishing American
The Stranger in Shakespeare
Being Busted
Collected Essays

FICTION

The Second Stone
Back to China
The Last Jew in America
Nude Croquet
The Messengers Will Come No More

THE RETURN OF

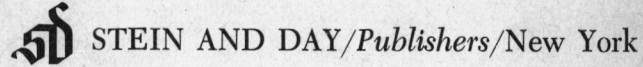 STEIN AND DAY/*Publishers*/New York

BY *Leslie A. Fiedler*

THE VANISHING

AMERICAN

First STEIN AND DAY PAPERBACK edition, 1969

First published in 1968
Copyright © 1968 by Leslie A. Fiedler
Library of Congress Catalog Card No. 68-15433
All rights reserved
Printed in the United States of America
Stein and Day/*Publishers*/Scarborough House
Briarcliff Manor, N.Y. 10510
ISBN 0-8128-1236-0

THIRD PRINTING 1976

WITH THANKS
TO
THE BLACKFOOT TRIBE
WHO
ADOPTED ME

"... let me devote my last words to those 'primitives' whose modest tenacity still offers us a means of assigning to human facts their true dimensions. Men and women who, as I speak, thousands of miles from here on some savannah ravaged by brush fire, or in some forest under torrential rain, are returning to camp to share a meagre pittance and to invoke their gods together; those Indians of the tropics and their counterparts throughout the world who have taught me their humble knowledge (in which is contained, nevertheless, the essence of the knowledge which my colleagues have charged me to transmit to others): soon, alas, they are all destined for extinction under the impact of illnesses and—for them even more horrible—modes of life with which we have plagued them. To them I have incurred a debt which I can never repay, even if, in the place in which you have put me, I were able to give some proof of the tenderness which they inspire in me and of the gratitude which I feel towards them by continuing to be as I was among them, and as, among you, I would hope never to cease from being: their pupil, their witness."

—FROM THE INAUGURAL LECTURE OF CLAUDE LÉVI-STRAUSS
AT THE COLLÈGE DE FRANCE, JANUARY 5, 1960

PREFACE

READERS OF MY earlier books will recognize that this volume marks the completion of a venture in literary anthropology to which I have been committed for more than a decade: an effort to define the myths which give a special character to art and life in America. This time, I have extended the boundaries of my inquiry backward to the mythical moment at which Atlantis disappeared—9,000 years before Solon—and forward to the perhaps equally mythical moment at which the Vanishing American has reappeared—right now.

With *Love and Death in the American Novel* and *Waiting for the End, The Return of the Vanishing American* constitutes a single work, the first of whose parts concerns itself with *eros* and *thanatos;* the second, with the hope of apocalypse and its failure; the third, with the Indian—all three, as I hope becomes clear in this volume, with that peculiar form of madness which dreams, and achieves, and *is* the true West.

I have tried out some of the ideas and themes of the present book before groups of students up and down the land, before my English Department colleagues here at Buffalo, and over the radio network of the Canadian Broadcasting Company. To all those who have listened and responded, I am grateful.

LESLIE A. FIEDLER
Buffalo, New York
July 4, 1967

CONTENTS

Introduction: The Demon of the Continent	11
Boxing the Compass	16
The World Without a West	29
The Basic Myths, I: The End of Petticoat Government	50
The Basic Myths, II: Love in the Woods	63
The Basic Myths, III: Two Mothers of Us All	84
The Basic Myths, IV: In Dreams Awake	109
The Failure of the Waking Dream	120
The Anti-Pocahontas of Us All	150
From Gary Cooper to Lee Marvin	159
The Higher Sentimentality	169
Index	188

INTRODUCTION:
THE DEMON OF THE CONTINENT

The moment the last nuclei of Red life break up in America, then the white man will have to reckon with the full force of the demon of the continent . . . within the present generation the surviving Red Indians are due to merge in the great white swamp. Then the Daimon of America will work overtly, and we shall see real changes.
    D. H. Lawrence, STUDIES IN CLASSIC AMERICAN LITERATURE

FIFTY YEARS AGO, the demonic future which Lawrence foresaw seemed only the troubled dream of a foreigner never really at home on our soil, a fantasy for poets to exploit and serious scholars to ignore; but suddenly his *then* is our *now*, and all of us seem men possessed.

Toward the end of Allen Ginsberg's hilarious little poem "America," for instance, the voice of that Jewish Walt Whitman from Paterson, New Jersey, mocking the fear of Russia which vexed the land in the mid-fifties, becomes suddenly the grunt of a stage Indian:

> The Russia want to eat us alive. The Russia's power
>   mad. She wants to take our cars from out our garages.
> Her want to grab Chicago. Her needs a Red Reader's
>   Digest. Her wants our auto plants in Siberia. Him
>   big bureaucracy running our filling stations.
> That no good. Ugh. Him make Indians learn read . . .

And at almost the same moment, Sebastian Dangerfield, J. P. Donleavy's alter ego in *The Ginger Man*, that joyous Irish-American extension of the methods of James Joyce, is yelling at the top of his fool voice, "Did you know I'm part Mohawk? *Whoo hoo!*"

It seems to make no difference at all, descendants of East European Jews or Dublin Irish, at home and abroad, everyone who thinks of himself as being in some sense an American feels the stirrings in him of a second soul, the soul of the Red Man—about which, not so very long ago, only an expatriate Englishman, his head full of Natty Bumppo and Chingachgook, had nerve enough to talk seriously. Young poets sign themselves "tribally yours," and lovers send each other feathers from ancient headdresses as tokens of esteem.

To be sure, the Indian has not disappeared at all "into the great White swamp," but has begun to reinvent himself—in part out of what remains of his own tribal lore, in part out of the mythology and science created by White men to explain him to themselves. The Native American Church, whose rites combine the smoking of peyote and the beating of drum with the recitatiton of formulae inherited from evangelical Protestantism, moves the Indians of the Southwest and West as nothing else has moved them since the Ghost Dance. And meanwhile, the Iroquois begin to learn, however reluctantly, to turn their backs on booze and the Baptists alike, and to take up the almost forgotten ceremonial of the Long House Religion.

Fascinatingly, it is not as Utes or Cheyennes, Mohawks or Delawares, that aboriginal Americans are rediscovering their identity, though once such parochial definitions constituted their whole sense of themselves and provided sufficient occasions for endless warfare. The Vanishing Americans may have bowed out as Last Mohicans or Flatheads or Sioux, but they return as what they all seemed to invading White Europeans from the start, simply "Indians," indistinguishable non-White others.

That Tuscarora leader of the Indian nationalist movement, Mad Bear, for instance, expounds to all who will listen a vision of Red America which begins in the legendary past of Atlantis and ends in the perhaps equally legendary future of after-the-Chinese-invasion. He explains how the ancestors of the Indian people once lived on a great island in the midst of the ocean, how they were wicked and therefore overwhelmed by a flood, how a tiny remnant escaped destruction by escaping through underground tunnels and an underground river which brought them up in the High Mesa country of the Hopis, how *all* Indians are descended from that remnant (whatever lies the White anthropologists may tell of movement over a land bridge from Asia). And he goes on to prophesy that times of trouble are ahead, indicated by the return to this world of the "Big People," sixty-foot giants, fourteen of whom are already stalking the land. He urges that it is the moment to take to the woods for council and, after "burning much tobacco," to begin the riots and demonstrations which, along with those sponsored by the Negroes, will lead to the intervention of the Chinese Communists and the destruction of all White Americans. After this, he assures his Indian listeners, the Negroes will depart in peace for Africa, whence they came, and the whole continent will be left to the Red Men who have inhabited it since the disappearance of Atlantis.

And even as the Indian has become visible once more to himself, he has become visible to certain White writers, who think of themselves as being on his side. Within a couple of years, Ed Dorn, a Black Mountain poet and voice of the sixties, has written a book about the Shoshone, and Edmund Wilson, last spokesman for the twenties, one about the Iroquois.

An astonishing number of novelists have begun to write fiction in which the Indian character, whom only yesterday we were comfortably bidding farewell (with a kind of security and condescension we can no longer even imagine), has disconcertingly reappeared. Books with Indians are, as any small boy can tell you "Western," and the Western we were sure up to a decade ago, had vanished along with the Indian into a region where no "serious reader" ventured: the world of pulp magazines, comic books, Class B movies, and innumerable second rate TV series, not even interesting as camp. And how certain we used to be, in that irrecoverable recent past, that the distinction between high literature and popular culture was final and beyond appeal: quite like that between White men and Indians, us and them.

But in the last several years, beginning somewhere around 1960, John Barth and Thomas Berger and Ken Kesey and David Markson and Peter Matthiessen and James Leo Herlihy and Leonard Cohen, as well as the inspired script writers of *Cat Ballou,* and I myself twice over, have, perhaps without being aware, been involved in a common venture: the creation of the New Western, a form which not so much redeems the Pop Western as exploits it with irreverence and pleasure, in contempt of the "serious reader" and his expectations.

Even Truman Capote's recent best-selling work of reportage, *In Cold Blood,* turns out to be an almost classic Western in theme, involving a white man and an Indian (Capote's Perry has a Cherokee mother, from whom he inherits his thick straight black hair and his "iodine-colored" skin) bound together in a homosexual alliance against the respectable White world around them; and the scene is westernmost Kansas, more Far West than Midwest, Capote himself remarks, with cattle and Stetson hats and Colorado just over the horizon. It is not just a lust for blood which has won a huge readership for that odd book, in which the author and history have so uncomfortably collaborated, but also a genuine hunger for the West.

That same hunger has recently impelled Norman Mailer to turn away from the metropolitan world that has long concerned him to the last frontier of Alaska. A key scene of his novel *What Are We Doing in Vietnam?* deals with the killing of a grizzly bear; and if this strikes us as warmed-over Hemingway rather than a venture into the New Western, Mailer may have redeemed himself by the ambiguous voice which tells his tale: perhaps that of a genuine WASP from Texas turned teenage disk jockey, perhaps that of a Harlem spade pretending he is so authentic and traditional a Westerner.

And though William Burroughs has so far done only a sketch or two in the Western mode, he keeps promising that his next book will represent "almost a deliberate change of style. I'm not sure if it's possible, but I want to try. I've been thinking about the western for years." So at least he assured an interviewer for the *Paris Review*, in 1965, promising that characters like Clem and Bradley Martin, Green Boy, Green Tony, Sammy the Butcher, and Willy the Fink (already worked out in his variants on science fiction) will appear in a Western scene, which will include "a lot of morphine addiction."

"Remember," he reminded his interviewer, "that there were a great many addicts at that time. Jesse James was an addict." And this surely will be something new in the world of the Western—if not for the scholar, certainly for those whose West has come to them via the pulps and TV.

The whole movement from Barth to Burroughs has, at any rate, raised two sets of important questions: some very general ones about the relationship between "high" and "low" art; and two quite specific ones about the genre involved—first, what is the Western in its classic or traditional form, and second, what precisely is new about the New Western?

BOXING
THE COMPASS

To BEGIN ANSWERING the first of these questions, we need only notice the fact, too obvious, perhaps, to have been properly observed or understood, that geography in the United States is mythological. From the earliest times, American writers have tended to define their own country—and much of our literature has, consequently, tended to define itself—topologically, as it were, in terms of the four cardinal directions: a mythicized North, South, East, and West. Correspondingly, there have always been four kinds of American books: Northerns, Southerns, Easterns, and Westerns, though we have been accustomed, for reasons not immediately clear, to call only the last by its name. Not all American books, of course, fit into one or another of these geographical categories, or even some canny blend of them; yet much of our most distinguished literature is thus mythologically oriented and can be fully appreciated only in this light.

The Northern tends to be tight, gray, low-keyed, underplayed, avoiding melodrama where possible—sometimes, it would seem, at all costs. Typically, its scene is domestic, an isolated household set in a hostile environment. The landscape is mythicized New England, "stern and rockbound," the weather deep winter: a milieu appropriate to the austerities and deprivations of Puritanism.

Here where the wind is always north-north-east
And children learn to walk on frozen toes . . .
Passion is here a soilure of the wits,
We're told, and love a cross for them to bear . . .

In the field of the novel, the Northern is represented, in general, by books easier to respect than to relish, since there is not much savor in them, books which could easily be thought of as *belles lettres,* fit for readers seeking loftier satisfactions than pleasure in a time when Christianity had been replaced by the Religion of Culture. The *other* novels of Harriet Beecher Stowe (*The Mayflower,* for instance, or *The Minister's Wooing*—the sort of thing she wrote when the demon which dictated *Uncle Tom's Cabin* deserted her) are a good instance of the type, as is most of William Dean Howells, a little of Henry James, and, supereminently, Edith Wharton's *Ethan Frome:* a dismal lot on the whole.

The Scarlet Letter is an apparent exception to these observations; it seems a *pre*-Northern, finally, describing the mythological origins of a world which wholly contains the later, true Northern. Actually, the Northern works better in verse than in prose, as a rule: in the narrative poems of Robert Frost, for instance, notably, say, "The Witch of Cöos"; in much of Edward Arlington Robinson, whose sonnet on New England is quoted above by way of illustration; and most recently in the work of Robert Lowell. One of its classics, however, is a prose poem in the form of a journal, Henry David Thoreau's *Walden,* which defines once and for all the archetypal essence of the transplanted lonely WASP in the midst of, or better, *against* the Massachusetts wilderness—in the course of which encounter, he becomes transformed into the Yankee. (But when he floated, somewhat earlier, at ease and with his brother for a companion, on the voyage whose diaries he made into *A Week on the Concord and Merrimack Rivers,* it is a Western he lived and wrote.)

The Southern, though its name is not quite so standardly used as that of the Western, is at least as well-known, perhaps too familiar to need definition at all. Certainly it is the most successful of all the topological subgenres of the novel in America, as triumphant on the highbrow level—from, say, Edgar Allan Poe through William Faulkner to Truman Capote or Flannery O'Connor—as on that of mass entertainment—from another side of that same Poe to Thomas Dixon's *The Clansman* (which suggested to D. W. Griffith the plot of *The Birth of a Nation*) or Margaret Mitchell's *Gone With the Wind* (the movie version of which leads an immortal life). The Southern has always challenged the distinction between High and Pop Art, since not merely Poe, its founder, but such latter-day successors of his as Faulkner and Capote have thrived in the two presumably sundered worlds of critical esteem and mass approval.

Perhaps this is because the Southern, as opposed to the Northern, does not avoid but seeks melodrama, a series of bloody events, sexual by implication at least, played out in the blood-heat of a "long hot summer" against a background of miasmal swamps, live oak, Spanish moss, and the decaying plantation house so dear to the hearts of moviemakers. Indeed, until there were ruined plantations—which is to say, until the Civil War, defeat, and Reconstruction—there could be no true Southern (Poe, being ante-bellum, had to imagine the doomed mansions appropriate to his horrors in a mythical Europe). The mode of the Southern is Gothic, American Gothic, and the Gothic requires a haunted house at its center. It demands also a symbolic darkness to cloak its action, a "blackness of darkness" which in the Old World was associated with the remnants of feudalism and especially with the dark-cowled ministers and "Black Nobility" of the Church.

What the Church and feudal aristocracy were for European Gothic, the Negro became for the American variety, "the Black," as he is mythologically called, being identified by that name with the nightmare terror which the writer of Southerns seeks to evoke, with the deepest guilts and fears of transplanted Europeans in a slaveholding community, or more properly, in a community which remembers having sent its sons to die in a vain effort to sustain slavery. But projecting those guilts and fears out upon the Blacks, draining himself of all his vital darkness, as it were, the European in the South condemned himself to a kind of mythological anemia; he became "Whitey."

Without the Negro, in any case, there is no true Southern. And whoever treated the Negro in our fiction—until urbanization changed everything—tended to write a Southern, whether he thought of himself as doing so or not; unless, of course, like Mark Twain in *Huckleberry Finn,* he turned his Negro protagonist into a Noble Savage, i.e. an Indian in blackface. Only where Jim is really a "nigger," i.e. at the very beginning and end of the novel where he plays the comic darky, or at certain points on the raft where he "camps" the role, addressing Huck as his "young master," does *Huckleberry Finn* become anything like a Southern; most of the way it is something quite other which we still have not defined. And occasionally it even threatens to become an Eastern, or a parody of one, when the Duke and the Dauphin bring their European pretensions aboard the raft; for the Eastern deals with the American confronting Europe, and cultural pretension is as essential to it as tourism.

Customarily, the Eastern treats the return of the American to the Old World (only then does he know for sure that he *is* an American), his Old Home, the place of origin of his old self, that original Adam, whom the New World presumably made a New Man. Its season is most appropriately spring, when the ice of New England symbolically breaks and all things seem—for a little while—possible; and, as is appropriate to that erotic time of year, it deals often with love (*The Roman Spring of Mrs. Stone* is the protypical title of one Eastern, the single novel of Tennessee Williams, who turned from his mythological South when he briefly forsook drama): the flirtation of the American, usually female, with the European, most often male. Sometimes, as in Henry James's *The Ambassadors,* the sexual-mythological roles are reversed, or, as in James Baldwin's *Giovanni's Room,* both are males, though one suspects Baldwin's Giovanni of being a Negro disguised as a European, and the book consequently of being a disguised Southern. In any event, the distribution of the sexes makes little difference in the Eastern, the encounter of European and American being doomed to frustration by the very nature of the case. This is so in part because the American turns out to be impelled by motives not so much truly erotic as merely anti-anti-erotic, and in part because, being not an émigré or a cosmopolitan but only a tourist (the Eastern is the form which defines the American precisely as a "tourist"), he—or, alternatively, she—has to go home.

It is Henry James (who may have sent his Lambert Strethers home, but who never returned to stay himself) whom we think of as the High Priest of the cult of the Eastern, or even as its Founder, though Nathaniel Hawthorne in *The Marble Faun,* and James Fenimore Cooper before him in *Homeward Bound,* were there first. Even so unadventurous a laureate of the middle classes as Henry Wadsworth Longfellow tried his hand at the Eastern, by implication in his verse translations and adaptations of European models, quite explicitly in such a novel as *Kavanaugh: A Tale.* But James began his career by asserting a claim to the form in *The American,* a claim which came to seem more and more exclusively his as he produced example after example (turning his hand to an occasional Northern like *The Bostonians* as a breather) until he could write no more. And with James—not so much originally as after his revival in the twenties—the Eastern became associated with that Culture Religion, so virulent in the United States between the two world wars.

Basic to that worship of High Art was the dogma that there are some books, in fiction chiefly those of James himself, an appreciation of which distinguishes the elect from the vulgar, the sensitive from the gross, and that those books can be known immediately because *a*) they are set in Europe, *b*) they mention other works of art, often so casually that only the cognoscenti know them without the the aid of footnotes, and *c*) they are written by expatriates. Obviously, most of the poetry of T. S. Eliot and much of Ezra Pound ("tourist" or Eastern poetry *par excellence*) falls into this category, quite in the style of their long unsuspected counterpart in the mid-nineteenth century—bound to them by many affinities besides a common love for Dante and a preference for being "abroad"—Longfellow himself.

Not all Easterns, however, belong in intention or in retrospect to the realm of self-conscious High Art; if any book which deals with the reaction of the American abroad (via tourism or dreams belongs to the genre, Mark Twain was one of its most assiduous practitioners, all the way from *Innocents Abroad* to *A Connecticut Yankee in King Arthur's Court*. And in our own century, we have had Scott Fitzgerald's *Tender is the Night*, a borderline case, perhaps, as well as most of the novels by Hemingway, who thought of himself, surely, as an emulator more of Twain than of James. But not everything is what it seems to a superficial scrutiny; and looking hard at Hemingway's *The Sun Also Rises* and *For Whom the Bell Tolls*, we discover that certain characters whom he represents as Spanish peasants seem mighty like Montana or Upper Michigan Indians—and that consequently he is actually writing, if not quite Westerns, at least crypto-Westerns, since it is the presence of the Indian which defines the mythological West.

The heart of the Western is not the confrontation with the alien landscape (by itself this produces only the Northern), but the encounter with the Indian, that utter stranger for whom our New World is an Old Home, that descendant of neither Shem nor Japheth, nor even, like the Negro imported to subdue the wild land, Ham. No grandchild of Noah, he escapes completely the mythologies we brought with us from Europe, demands a new one of his own. Perhaps he was only a beast of the wildwood, the first discoverers of America reassured themselves, not human at all; and at the end of the fifteenth century, Princes of the Church gravely discussed whether, being undescended from Adam, the Indian indeed had a soul like our own. It was a question by no means settled once and for all when the Church answered "yes"; for at the beginning of our own century, Lawrence amended that answer to "yes, but—" Yes, a soul, but *not* one precisely like our own, except as our own have the potentiality of becoming like his.

And in the five hundred years between, how the Indian in his ultimate otherness has teased and baffled the imagination of generation after generation of European voyagers and settlers. How they have tried to assimilate him to more familiar human types, to their own mythologic stock-in-trade. The name "Indian" itself memorializes the first misguided effort of Columbus to assure himself that he was in those other, those *East* Indies, after all, and confronting nothing but types known since Marco Polo, like the inhabitants of Cipango or Cathay.

After that delusion had collapsed, after the invention as opposed to the mere discovery of America, there were new explainers-away eager to identify the Red Men with the Welsh, the Irish—and especially the Semites, the lost Tribes of Israel.

Only the minority group comprising "scientific" anthropologists have clung in our time to the delusion of Columbus, postulating a migration from continent to continent which makes our Indians kin to the subjects of the Great Khan after all. And only a handful of nuts have been willing to identify the Indians as survivors of quite another world, another creation—refugees from Atlantis or Mu. Lawrence was tempted to the latter alternative, hinting somewhat mysteriously of an affinity between the western Indians, at least, and the priesthood of the lost Pacific civilization, "the world once splendid in the fulness of the other way of knowledge."

"They seem to lie under the last spell of the Pacific influence," he says of the Redskins of Cooper's *The Prairie;* "they have the grace and physical voluptuousness . . . of the lands of the great Ocean." But the deep imagination of

Americans has sought stubbornly to link the Savages of the New World with the once-Chosen People of the Old.

From those apostles to the Indians of the seventeenth century who thought of themselves as penetrating the wilderness to restore the Old Testament to those to whom it properly belonged, through Fenimore Cooper in the early nineteenth, recounting the adventures of just such a deluded missionary in the form of Parson Amen in *Oak Openings* (to whom the bewildered Redskins object that, being Indians, they can never be *lost*), to the later Mormons, incorporating the wrong-headed myth in their homemade scriptures, and the rancher of *Cat Ballou,* baffled at the Indian who refuses to answer his Hebrew greeting of "*Shalom!*"—the tradition has never died.

It is, in fact, carried from door to door even now by missionaries for the Church of Latter Day Saints, who leave behind them the *Book of Mormon,* complete with a prefatory gloss that sends those eager to know the "Fate of Indians" to the fourteenth verse of the thirteenth chapter of *First Nephi:*

> And it came to pass that I beheld multitudes of the Gentiles upon the land of promise; and I beheld the wrath of God, that it was upon the seed of my brethren; and they were scattered before the Gentiles and were smitten.

This may be, to true believers, a sufficient mythological explanation not only of the origin, but of the expropriation of the Indians. To the Indians themselves, however, though they may be in fact as stubborn and persistent witnesses as the Jews, it remains inconceivable that they can be anything so familiar to the three thousand-year-old tradition of the White West as mere children of Israel, that they can be anything but their untranslatable selves.

Everything else which belongs to the Western scene has long since been assimilated: the prairies subdivided and landscaped; the mountains staked off as hunting preserves and national parks; fabulous beasts, like the grizzlies and the buffalo, killed or fenced in as tourist attractions; even the mythological season of the Western, that nonexistent interval between summer and fall called "Indian summer," become just another part of the White year. Only the Indian survives, however ghetto-ized, debased, and debauched, to remind us with his alien stare of the new kind of space in which the baffled refugees from Europe first found him (an unhumanized vastness), and the new kind of time through which, despite all our efforts, he still moves (a historyless antiquity). It is for this reason that tales set in the West seem to us not quite Westerns, unfulfilled occasions for myth rather than myth itself, when no Indian —"stern and imperturbable warrior" or lovely, complaisant squaw, it scarcely matters—appears in them.

The Western story in archetypal form is, then, a fiction dealing with the confrontation in the wilderness of a transplanted WASP and a radically alien other, an Indian—leading either to a metamorphosis of the WASP into something neither White nor Red (sometimes by adoption, sometimes by sheer emulation, but *never* by actual miscegenation), or else to the annihilation of the Indian (sometimes by castration-conversion or penning off into a ghetto, sometimes by sheer murder). In either case, the tensions of the encounter are resolved by eliminating one of the mythological partners —by ritual or symbolic means in the first instance, by physical force in the second. When the first method is used, possibilities are opened up for another kind of Western, a secondary Western dealing with the adventures of that New Man, the American *tertium quid;* but when the second is employed—our homegrown Final Solution—the Western disappears as a living form, for the West has, in effect, been made into an East.

But into what exactly is the transplanted European converted by the Western encounter when he resists resolving it by genocide? It is easy enough to name the aspects of Americans defined by the three other forms: the Northern, in which we become Yankees; the Southern, in which we are turned into Whitey; the Eastern, in which we are revealed as Tourists. But the transformation effected in the Western evades easy definition. Thinking of Natty Bumppo (that first not-quite-White man of our literature, for all his boasts about having "no cross in my blood") and his descendants, we are tempted to say that it is the woodsman which the ex-European becomes beside his Red companion: the hunter, the trapper, the frontiersman, the pioneer, at last the cowboy—or maybe only next-to-last, for after him comes the beatnik, the hippie, one more wild man seeking the last West of Haight-Ashbury in high-heeled boots and blue jeans. But even as he ceases to be beatnik and becomes fully hippie, the ultimate Westerner ceases to be White at all and turns back into the Indian, his boots becoming moccasins, his hair bound in an Indian headband, and a string of beads around his neck—to declare that he has fallen not merely out of Europe, but out of the Europeanized West, into an aboriginal and archaic America.

It is tempting, at this point, to take the dilemma as the answer, and to settle for saying that, since this new kind of man came into existence only with the West, he is best called simply the "Westerner," that there is no way of moving beyond this. But we know, too, that at the moment of looking into the eyes of the Indian, the European becomes the "American" as well as the Westerner. And if we forget it for a moment, there is the title of Henry James's early novel to remind us: his account of a white barbarian from San Francisco, actually called—with a bow to Columbus—Christopher Newman. And who has more right than the man from the farthest West to be called both new and American, since before a single White man had set foot on American soil, the whole continent had been dreamed by Europe as "the West": a legendary place beyond or under the ocean wave, a land of the dead or those who rise from the dead. And it needed only the invention of the name America to set up the equation *America equals the West*.

Once the Atlantic was crossed, moreover, the name *West* was transferred, step by step, to whatever part of the continent lured men on just over the line of settlement, to the unexplored space behind the next natural barrier, past the Appalachians, the Mississippi, the Rockies. Vermont or Maine may define our North once and for all; Georgia, Alabama, or Louisiana may circumscribe our mythological South; the harbors of Boston and New York City, ports from which tourists embark for the adventure of returning to the Old World, can scarcely be thought of as anything but the East.

But where, geographically, is the elusive West? We know that first of all it was Virginia itself, the Old Dominion, then New England, Pennsylvania, Kentucky, Louisiana, Ohio, Missouri, Texas, the Oregon Territory, etc., etc.—always a bloody ground just over the horizon, or just this side of it, where we confronted *in their own territory* the original possessors of the continent.

So long as a single untamed Indian inhabits it, any piece of American space can become to the poet's imagination an authentic West, as the small Vermont town of Acton was transformed, even in the twentieth century, by the vision of Robert Frost's extraordinary poem "The Vanishing Red." Beginning with the lines: "He is said to have been the last Red Man in Acton. And the Miller is said to have laughed . . ." it ends by becoming a parable of the war to the death between White Man and Red, though Frost pretends, ironically, to refuse to tell it:

> It's too long a story to go into now.
> You'd have to have been there and lived it.
> Then you wouldn't have looked on it just as a matter
> Of who began it between the two races.

It is, however, only a desperate sort of Last Western, a hymn to the end of one more West, that Frost manages to write, as seems appropriate to our time. For, by and large, we have used up the mythological space of the West along with its native inhabitants, and there are no new places for which we can light out ahead of the rest—even Alaska being only a fiftieth state. Can we reestablish the West anywhere at all, then? This is the question that troubles certain of our writers, eager to dream the old American dreams. The earth, it turns out, is mythologically as well as geographically round; the lands across the Pacific will not do, since on the rim of the second ocean, West becomes East, our whole vast land (as Columbus imagined, and Whitman nostalgically remembered at the opening of the Suez Canal) a Passage to India.

Maybe the moon will serve our purposes, or Mars; maybe up and out will turn out to be a true archetypal equivalent to the Way West, as we have already begun to surmise, calling some of the literature of space adventure "space operas," on the model of "horse operas," which is to say, Westerns. But unless "stern and imperturbable" Martians await us, or lovely and complaisant lady Lunatics—as certain makers of science fiction have already tried to assure us —whom we can assimilate to our old myths of the Indian, Outer Space will not seem an extension of our original America, the America which shocked and changed Europe, but a second, a meta-America, which may shock and change us. On our shores, the myth of the West which had teased the European imagination up to the time of Dante—the myth of an unattainable and unpeopled world—was altered into one of a world open to "plantation," but inhabited by hostile aliens: a myth so deeply rooted in us that, in spite of scientific testimony to the contrary, we insist on imagining the New Worlds we now approach inhabited by natives, "savages" benign or threatening.

We have defined the "territory ahead" for too long in terms of the mythologies created out of our meeting with and response to the Indians to abandon them without a struggle. They have proved sufficiently adaptable to describe our relations with Negroes and Polynesians, with all colored peoples, in fact (Twain's Nigger Jim and Melville's Queequeg are mythological blood brothers, after all, to Cooper's Chingachgook); and we dream of taking those same terms with us into a future not quite so terrifying and unfamiliar as it sometimes seems, if only they will work there, too.

THE WORLD
WITHOUT A WEST

FOR A LONG TIME, Europeans thought of themselves as inhabiting a world without a West: a three-fold *oecumene* made up of Europe itself, Asia, and Libya, which is to say a ruling and redeemed North plus a subsidiary and redeemable East and South. The fourth direction they considered closed off to colonization and the hope of salvation by the impassable barrier of the River Ocean, which could be glimpsed through the terminal Straits of Gibraltar or from the shores of those peripheral European Isles, Ireland and Iceland. This notion was present in the poetic cosmogony of Herodotus; the ancient mythologizing geographers passed it on to their Christian opposite numbers, who, finding it symbolically apt, converted it into an article of faith. Had not the ancient Jews themselves spoken of the three sons of Noah inheriting three worlds, Semitic, Japhetic, and Hamitic? And were not those royal magicians who came to greet the infant Jesus three in number, arriving as they did each from one of the three major sectors of the earth? And was not three, finally and most convincingly, the number of the Holy Trinity itself and therefore properly inscribed in God's second Book of Revelations, the great globe of the world?

The belief is formally represented in the Pope's threefold miter, which signifies his ecumenical sway over the triple *orbis terrarum;* and it was explicitly argued by St. Augustine, who decided that, even if there were a fourth quarter of the world, it could not possibly be a territory inhabited or inhabitable by those for whom Christ had died, but only a watery waste banned to all but spirits, subhuman or superhuman.

Though Europeans were content—even, after a while, obliged by doctrine—to think of their private lives and common history as acted out in a tripartite world, in dreams they sought from the start the forbidden and impossible fourth quarter of the globe. Excluded from geography and history, the West persisted as fantasy, legend, a place to be sought inside the skull of ordinary dreamers or inspired poets. In the earliest Greek writings, it is already the region of ghosts rather than living men: "the Islands of the Blest by deep eddying Ocean . . . ," "where no snow falls, no strong winds blow and there is never any rain. . . ." The names vary, but the essential concept remains the same on both sides of Christianity; what Homer and Hesiod described to themselves as the Isles of the Blest or Elysium becomes the Hesperides, the Fortunate Isles, eventually the Earthly Paradise. Where else except in the direction of the setting sun can one look for the Great Good Place beyond death, the region where what survives of the human spirit bides forever or awaits resurrection?

And it is the Celts, the Irish in particular, who, from their home on the very verge of the West, have dreamed most variously and convincingly of that other Place, naming it Tir-nan-Og, and Tir-nam-Beo, Mag Mon and Mag Mell, at last Avalon: the island of apple trees where Good King Arthur sleeps and awaits his second coming. D. H. Lawrence writes:

> These races have remained true to some principle . . . which has had no place in the European Christian-social scheme. Therefore they placed themselves in a polarity with the great invisible force of America, they looked to . . . the land of the setting sun, over the great sea to the unknown America. Their heaven was the land under the western wave, the Celtic Tir na Og [sic].

From Iceland, the first real expedition may have set sail for the West, actually debarking in present-day Brooklyn, which improbably became—for imaginations still trapped in the dream dreamed by Isidore of Seville, a land where no snow falls and "self-sowing wheat" springs up without human intervention, Vinland the Good.

But it is from that other penultimate Isle, from Ireland, that the mind of Europe takes its first American trip in the fictional *Voyage of Bran,* a poem probably composed somewhere around the year 700 A.D., whose pagan hero becomes (the interconnections are traced in an intriguing study by Geoffrey Ashe called *Land to the West*), in the transmogrifications and permutations of myth, St. Brendan-Brandan, a later legendary explorer of the West, as well as Barinthus his guide, and perhaps also the shadowy Sir Brons who appears beside Joseph of Arimathea in the story of the Holy Grail.

The name Bran means "raven" (and a raven sits, in traditional iconography, on the shoulder of the corresponding saint): the bird which Old Testament legend tells us Noah sent forth first and inconclusively to search for a New World in the watery waste left by the Flood. And Columbus, of course, means "dove": Noah's second bird-emissary, which did, indeed, return with the olive branch as the sign of a landfall. It is a coincidence too lovely and mysterious not to notice; but no Christian commentator (not even that fantastic latter-day exegete, D. H. Lawrence) has paused to reflect on how *Genesis* VIII can be read as symbolic prophecy to the two discoveries—via the dream trip and the sea voyage—of America: "And he sent forth a raven, which went forth to and fro, until the waters were dried up from off the earth. And also he sent a dove from him, to see if the waters were abated. . . . And the dove came in to him in the evening, and, lo, in her mouth was an olive leaf plucked off: so Noah knew that the waters were abated from off the earth."

What has stayed in the mind of Ireland, passing from

there to the general European imagination, is Bran's vision of the happy land in the West, a link between certain outlawed myths of the pagan past and the Christian legend to come:

> There is a distant isle . . .
> Lovely land through the world's age,
> On which many blossoms drop . . .
> There is nothing rough nor harsh,
> But sweet music striking on the ear.
> Without grief, without sorrow, without death.

And this becomes St. Brendan's "land of Promise" only three hundred years later; it blends, that is to say, into visions of the Terrestrial Paradise which Judaeo-Christian tradition had placed at "the end of the East." All that is necessary to make Celtic and Christian fantasy one is to realize that the earth is mythologically as well as geographically round, that the paradise lost in the East can be regained by sailing West.

Outside of Ireland, however, there are obstacles in the way of such an identification. On the one hand, the West which was in the process of being revealed as America had been traditionally conceived as the place of escape from pain and death, the infinitely desirable land; on the other, it had been portrayed as the forbidden garden, the haven denied to fallen man by a just God, a paradise lost irrevocably as long as human history endured. This is a notion congenial to Christian orthodoxy, but much older than its dogmas.

Even the legend of Atlantis as retold (or invented?) in the *Timaeus* and *Critias* of Plato is not merely the myth of a vast world to the West, a kind of space which dwarfs the Mediterranean *oecumene* ("the island was larger than Libya and Asia put together, and was the way to other islands, and from these you might pass to the whole of the opposite continent which surrounded the true ocean . . ."), but is also the account of a prehistoric fall of man, nine thousand years before Solon, which begins with the defeat of Atlantis in all its pride at the hands of proto-Athenians, and ends in the disappearance of the great kingdom beneath the sea. And this event is explained twice over as the gods' device to bar Europe from the West, as well as to punish the inhabitants of the lost land for their sins: once in the *Timaeus* ("For which reason the sea in those parts is impassable and impenetrable, because there is a shoal of mud in the way . . ."), and again in the unfinished *Critias* ("Atlantis . . . when afterwards sunk by an earthquake, became an impassable barrier of mud to voyagers sailing from hence to any part of the ocean").

All the more, then, did later Christian commentators, for whom Plato's fable is reinforced by the Biblical legend of the expulsion from Eden, emphasize the theme of a garden-world lost by a fall from virtue—even St. Brendan being forbidden the interior of the "land of Promise," on whose beaches he had landed—with the promise that some day God would open it to all of his elect.

The classic expression of medieval orthodoxy's acceptance of a permanent exclusion from the West is to be found in Ulysses' long speech in Canto XXVI of Dante's *Inferno:* in part an extrapolation from the *Navigatio Sancti Brendani,* in part a simultaneous prophecy and rejection of the age of exploration still a couple of hundred years ahead.

No more trinitarian mind than Dante's ever existed; the tripartite *oecumene* was as symbolically necessary to his sense of himself as a citizen of this world as the *terza rima* was to his sense of himself as a poet singing the terrors and rewards of the three worlds beyond. Yet a dream of actually entering the fourth world, of taking the West by storm, also possessed him, though he was deeply aware that all the major pieties of life here and now (themselves threefold) militated against such an attempt: "the sweetness of having a son . . . duty to an old father . . . the legitimate love that should have made Penelope rejoice. . . ." And he put the passionate declaration of the doomed ardor which cues such a dream, as well as the evocation of the obligations which should have dampened it, in the mouth of Ulysses, that wanderer out of the remotest European past who becomes in Dante's late medieval imagination the First American.

Seven hundred years later, Ezra Pound acknowledged the justice of the mythological indentification by taking to himself the name of the Greek hero shipwrecked in the world of myth. But Pound's Ulysses reverses the final pilgrimage Dante attributed to him, returning to Europe from where the West ends, on the shabby streets of Hailey, Idaho:

> His true Penelope was Flaubert,
> He fished by obstinate isles.

It is all there from the start, however: an old man, impatient of restraint, whipping on his equally ancient comrades, who pause in terror at the Pillars of Hercules ("those straits where Hercules set up his signs, so that man should go no further"), at what seems to them the ultimate West but is only the end of the old East, the mere vestibule to the new and true West ("the experience, following the sun, of the world without people").

Into Ulysses' very exhortation, Dante has woven metaphors of blasphemy and horror, since, after all, the Greek leader is recapitulating his adventure in Hell: "turned our backs upon the morning . . . made our oars into wings for that mad flight . . . always pressing toward the left. . . ." The poet wants to leave no doubt in the minds of his readers that Ulysses' voyage was a left-handed, ill-omened, sinister conquest ("acquistando" is the word Dante puts in his mouth to describe his tabooed progress): a turning away from the direction out of which the sun rises, signifying salvation, to the direction into which it sets, signifying death; a flight compared by implication to the fatal course of Phaeton. But more than ill-omened or fatal, it is *mad*, since to enter the West is to try to live in a dream, i.e., to go insane. This is why, from the time of Columbus on, the charge first made in a poem has been repeated over and over again in history, each new penetration of unpeopled space labeled, like each one before, mad, mad, mad! Yet in the Ulysses Canto at least, the crazy attempt is made, and seems—for one tremulous moment—to have attained not disaster, but a vision of alien splendor, caught in three beautiful lines:

> Tutte le stelle già dell'altro polo
> vedea la notte, e 'l nostro tanto basso,
> che non surgea fuor del marin suolo.

("Already the night beheld the other pole's whole panoply of stars, and ours so low it barely rose above the ocean's sill.")

Upreared from that strange sea into that strange sky, an even stranger land appears, an island-mountain, impossibly lofty and still so distant when first spied that it seems a dusky no-color. We know from the context that it is the island of Purgatory, surmounted by the Terrestrial Paradise, which Ulysses and his men have come upon; but how hard it is to believe this bleak unfeatured world has anything in common with the Green Garden on the Hill which the poet is to describe in the *Purgatorio*. Yet it *is* land and stirs joy in the hearts of the voyagers—a joy turned swiftly woe, as a whirlwind strikes and the ship is turned three times about, the fourth time sucked under (how appropriately the symbolic numbers occur—the sacred three, the forbidden four); "as it pleased Another," Ulysses-Dante observes, then concludes, "so that the sea closed over us again." It is a phrase briefer, but not unlike the cadence that brings Melville's later epic poem, this time entirely about America, to its end: ". . . and the great shroud of the sea rolled on as it rolled five thousand years ago."

In Dante, to be sure, we are dealing—the scholars hasten to remind us—with allegory; we must, therefore, understand that what he portrays as doomed to shipwreck is no actual venture in wooden bottoms out into the Unknown, but that lust to know everything, that Faustian passion which is to make the Renaissance. Yet the literal story moves us (more than almost any episode in the *Inferno*, except for the stories of Paolo and Francesca and of Count Ugolino in his terrible tower) on another level, seeming the prototype of all those tales in Hakluyt and Purchas, and of the real voyages which prompted them; as the ambivalence already strong on both sides in Dante's good European heart tilted toward the positive pole in those who followed him. In Dante, the medieval mind says its elegant last word on an event it could imagine but not achieve, yearn for but not applaud, since for that mind the opening of the West, the discovery of America, did not stand for but *was* a sin, a fall into terrible freedom.

In a sense, we have felt this all the more intensely since Columbus did what Dante only dreamed and damned to Hell, though we, of course, find it in retrospect a breakthrough elating rather than dismaying. Edmundo O'Gorman, in an extraordinary little book called *The Invention of America,* tries to remind us of what we find it easier and easier to forget: that the myth of the penetration of the West, the emergence of Europe into a realm of freedom it had long feared, is not less mythically potent when converted from poetry to history. "It was the Spanish part of the invention of America," he writes, "that liberated Western man from the fetters of a prisonlike conception of his physical world" —teaching him, O'Gorman might have added, though he prefers to leave this implicit, that "sin" is often the name which the past gives to the future; or, alternatively, that just as the history of the Old World begins mythologically with a *felix culpa,* a happy fault that led to expulsion from the Earthly Paradise, so the history of the New World begins with the second happy fault of trying to reenter Paradise with the aid of sail and compass and human daring.

Certainly the same myth that moved poets to verses moved Columbus to action. He liked to speak, in the days when he walked the world trying to stir up support for his expedition, of tales of the West told him by old sailors; but what seems really to have fired his imagination were the same sources which Dante had drawn on for his Ulysses Canto: Plato's pseudo-reminiscence of Atlantis; the half-mythological speculations of those early geographers, Macrobius and Isidore of Seville; as well as the verses of earlier poets, perhaps the *Navigatio* of St. Brendan itself, and, in any event, certain "prophetic" verses from Seneca's *Medea*.

In the apology for his father which Columbus' son Ferdinand published as a factual account of his life—though it begins with a faked noble pedigree and ends with a vain attempt to prove that Columbus knew all along he had really discovered America—Ferdinand reminds his readers of those verses ("There will come a time in later years, when Ocean shall loosen the bonds by which we have been confined, when an immense land shall be revealed and Tiphys shall disclose new worlds, and Thule shall no longer be Ultima Thule, the furthest of lands"); and he concludes gravely, "Now it is considered certain that this prophecy was fulfilled in the person of the Admiral."

What most modern historians consider certain, however, is that "the Admiral" himself was quite unaware of having fulfilled any such prophecy, though it is barely possible that Columbus may deliberately have lied (as his son seems to imply) about the lands he had found, considering it strategically preferable to locate them in a mythological East rather than a mythological West. Certainly "East" meant to his potential backers the "Indies," and their inexhaustible mines of gold; and thinking of the region he had attained as East rather than West would tend to conceal even from himself (cautious and exaggeratedly pious Marrano that he was) the blasphemous nature of his quest. There is no doubt, at any rate, that like the poets of antiquity and their Christian imitators from St. Brendan to Dante, he dreamed of a Paradisal Isle at the end of the Ocean, in what could equally well be described as the Far West or "the end of the East."

It is common belief that Columbus, stumbling on our land, thought himself in Cipango and Cathay; few somehow remember—perhaps because no such place is to be found on any map that survives in our heads—that he was also convinced that he had discovered the Earthly Paradise itself. In his famous "Letter to the Sovereigns," he contends that the Orinoco River, whose mouth he found, was actually the Gihon, one of the four rivers which the Bible tells us flow out of Eden, and that the fresh water mingled with the salt sea of the Gulf he rode "may well come from Paradise." He has some doubts, he confesses to his royal audience, since the coast on which he had touched could only have been the remote perimeter of Paradise, the Garden of Eden presumably lying "far inland." Yet at the end of all his self-questioning, he concludes: "I deeply feel within me that there, where I have said, lies the Terrestrial Paradise."

Judaeo-Christian mythology had insisted that man was barred—if not forever, at least until the redemption of the world—from that garden spot where he began. How extraordinary, then, to have reached even its perimeter, and how doubly strange to have discovered in that world, presumably unpeopled since the sin of Adam, naked creatures who looked like men—and who lived, in its kindly clime, lives which seemed at first glance nearly paradisal. Merely to have discovered the dreamed-of land in the West was disturbing enough, but to have found it not at all a *mondo senza gente*, as Augustine had taught and Dante believed, was a culture shock from which it took Europe centuries to recover. In the rendering of the scene by Columbus' son Ferdinand, the wonder of that first encounter still survives:

> At daybreak they saw an island . . . full of green trees and abounding in springs . . . and inhabited by a multitude of people who hastened to the shore, astounded and marveling at the sight of the ships, which they took for animals. These people could hardly wait to see what sort of things the ships were. The Christians were no less eager to know what manner of people they had to do with. . . .

"What manner of people." There is the question which was to vex Europe long and hard, though at first Columbus seems to have had no trouble accommodating them to his inherited ethnic mythology. After all, they were nothing more nor less than "Indians," i.e., inhabitants of those Indies of whose existence he had long been aware, and whose fabled treasures he had come seeking. To be sure, these particular "Indians" were much more naive and childlike than earlier reports had indicated, but all the better as far as trade and amicable relations were concerned! ". . . the Admiral, perceiving they were a gentle, peaceful, and very simple people, gave them little red caps and glass beads which they hung about their necks, together with other trifles that they cherished as if they were precious stones of great price."

Even after the first comic-pathetic drawing of blood ("They had no arms like ours, nor knew thereof; for when the Christians showed them a naked sword, they foolishly grasped it by the blade and cut themselves"), Columbus seemed not a bit put off, proceeding on schedule to teach them his own tongue and to recruit wives for his men from among them—in both of which efforts he reported things to have gone satisfactorily.

To be sure, Columbus soon heard scary stories about the fabulous Caribs, from whose tribal name the word "cannibal" was derived, since they were reputed to castrate, fatten, and eat their captives. But this ferocious variety of "Indian" always turned out to be somewhere else, in the next island or the next—quite like the gold for which he kept inquiring hopefully. Perhaps both stories were fictions, games the Indians played with their white invaders. Yet Columbus remained undismayed by the tall tales, as he was to remain undismayed by grimmer trials: the appearance of syphilis as an unexpected dowry from his men's native wives; the squabbles which divided them against each other, involving those wives and other matters; occasional attacks by newly encountered Indians, or those who had learned from experience the meaning of cold steel.

The really disturbing threat of the Indian, technologically backward and eternally surprised at the White man's treachery, was never military—nor even, despite the unexpectedness of the pox, venereal—but mythological, which is to say, based not on what he did, only on what he was. So long as he was taken as an Asiatic, this threat did not operate, as it did not operate for Columbus; but once Cathay-Paradise had been recognized as America, a New Found Land, and its inhabitants as problematic aliens, the damage was done.

If the inhabitants of the world opened by Columbus are not "Indians," troubled Europeans began to ask themselves, what are they? Corresponding to the three parts of the old *oecumene* are the three tribes descended from Noah's three sons, Shem, Ham, and Japheth; but the natives of America belong to none of the three, so how then can they be considered children of Adam, which is to say, men, at all? Do they—in terms of Christian mythology—have souls? Can they, *must* they (for the obligation follows, if they are granted souls still unredeemed) be saved?

Very soon after the time of Columbus' voyages, a debate on this subject reached the highest councils of the Roman Catholic church, in the passionate arguments between Bartolomé de las Casas (especially urgent because he believed the end of the world imminent, and the salvation of the Indians a pre-condition) and Juan Ginés de Sepúlveda. Implicit in the subject was the question of slavery; for once the Indian—or any other colored man—was denied a soul, he could be condemned to a life of servitude quite as if he were a steer or an ox, and "that peculiar institution" so distinctive of America, a form of servitude to which one is condemned by the color of his skin, was ready to be invented.

It was left to the mind of Northern Europe, however, to take the final step in this direction (since the Church decided that, after all, Indians do have souls); and for that mind the secular scriptures of essays, poems, and plays were much more important than priestly exegesis of Biblical texts: in particular Montaigne's essay "On the Cannibals" and Shakespeare's late play, *The Tempest,* which begins by seeming to echo Montaigne and ends by attempting to refute him. Like de las Casas and Sepúlveda, they are ideal, polar opponents; and like the earlier pair, it is really the question of slavery they are arguing—though this is not at all clear until one has passed from Montaigne to Shakespeare, from an exaggerated and explicit defense of Indian ways of life to a violent attack on the whole Indian race, disguised as a Mystery Play.

Once a European Christian has granted the American Indian full human status, he has the choice either of trying to Christianize him, i.e., to complete or perfect his humanity, or of recognizing his "paganism" as an alternate way of life, an equal though totally other human possibility. The White thinker, that is to say, who extends his definition of the human to include the Indian, finds himself becoming either (like de las Casas) a missionary or (like Montaigne) an anthropologist, falling prey either to the Spanish passion or to the French. Just as it can be shown that the clerisy of Spain was thrown into a missionary frenzy by the reports of the early explorers, so it can be demonstrated that the French intellectual community was shocked into a kind of scientific cultural relativism by the first accounts of Indian life, that even in Montaigne (*"chacun appelle barbarie ce qui n'est pas de son usage . . ."*) the seeds of the *Encyclopédie* are already germinating. Reflecting on the Indians of "la France Antarctique," which is to say, present day Brazil, he reacts like a true scientist confronted with a new subject for study; he recognizes, in fact, that the invention of America implies the invention of a new science: the systematic investigation of the *other* man, the *other* culture.

Like a good anthropologist, at any rate, he collects native songs and artifacts, engages in conversations with returned explorers and recently imported "native informants"—attempts finally to define and specify a difference without prejudging it. If anything, he leans over backward trying to escape his own cultural limitations; he permits himself to become enamored of a paradox which almost betrays him into the sort of sentimental self-hatred we associate with Rousseau: civilization is more savage, more barbarous than nature, natural man the real gentleman. There is moreover, something a little pathological in the relish with which Montaigne recounts the details of Indian cannibalism, lingering over the eating of human flesh almost—almost—as if recommending it, though he purports to be defending it only as the extreme form of his paradox.

North Americans do not ordinarily recall that for a long time after Columbus, and especially in the Latin mind to which he first spoke, "Indian" quite simply equaled "cannibal." Anglo-Saxons, on the other hand, tend to associate the eating of human flesh with Africans or Fijians, Negroes or Melanesians—Black men, at any rate, rather than Red. For settlers in the English colonies, *scalping* quite soon became the utterly alien offense of the aborigines, though, in truth, it seems not to have been an Indian custom at all until the White Man began offering bounties for slain enemies.

Yet what initially rose up out of the deep imagination of Europeans, released from imageless repression by the news of savages consuming each other in the Antipodes, was a buried longing for the taste of human flesh—not quite sublimated even by the symbolic eating of the Christian Man-God in the Mass. That this had begun to stir in the under-mind of medieval man, Dante's *Inferno* testifies; for the third of its most poignant passages—those three camouflaged protests against the system the poem pretends to celebrate, which, precisely for that reason, have most moved his readers, pious and impious alike—opens with a view of Count Ugolino gnawing the skull of his enemy, the Archbishop, and ends with his ambiguous revelation that—perhaps, perhaps—he had been driven to eat the flesh of his own sons. *"Poscia, più che 'l dolor, poté 'l digiuno"* (then hunger proved more strong than sorrow).

In Shakespeare the "hunger more strong than sorrow" loses its mythological force; for though in *The Tempest* he creates the very name of his monster-villain, Caliban, by anagrammatizing the word "cannibal," cannibalism plays no part in the plot—nor for that matter does scalping. The one has begun to recede into the past; the other lies still in the future. What functions for Shapespeare's imagination is sex, or more specifically rape—another offense which later

Anglo-Saxon fantasy transferred from Red Man to Black. Indeed, Caliban *is* a little Black, his mother from "Argier," which is to say, "Algiers," part of that Moorish world from which Othello came, as well as Aaron, the villain who haunts the rape-ridden play *Titus Andronicus.*

But his *nègritude* constitutes only the smallest part of Caliban's mythological being. He is also in part Indian— born of a fusion of Montaigne's Brazilians, Pigafetta's Patagonian "giants" (whose god, the companion of Magellan recorded, was called Setebos—like Caliban's and his mother's), and the natives of the Bermudas. Indeed, for all of Shakespeare's pretense of moving it to the Mediterranean, Caliban's island *is* one of those "stormy Bermoothes," some three or four accounts of which Shakespeare seems to have read—all written by survivors of shipwreck on their subtropical shores. Storm-girdled yet benign, it must have seemed to Shakespeare the tabooed island paradise of Dante, miraculously released from its long ban, though in the end a delusion and a cheat.

But Caliban is not merely a Moor plus a Brazilian-Patagonian-Bermudan Indian; he is also in part a fish—as befits the inhabitant of a hemisphere scholars had long believed all water—or more precisely perhaps, a sea-creature that had made it onto shore, finding himself at home in the mud flats, since he, too, was compounded chiefly of the baser elements, earth and water. All of this, however, amounts to saying that he is, finally and essentially, a monster: a hybrid halfway between man and beast, that *homme sauvage* who had begun to haunt the dreams of Europe long before the discovery of America.

To Shakespeare, in fact, the Indian is quite simply that Savage Man; all the rest is trimming, historical and ethnographic embellishment. From the time he wrote *Love's Labour's Lost* at the very beginning of his career to the moment of composing *The Tempest* toward the end, Shakespeare typically qualified the "man of Inde" as rude or savage.

The Savage Man is associated with sexual assault rather

than cannibalism. He can be read, indeed, as a projection, out of the darkness of the European mind, of all in man's passionate nature which resisted not only the bonds of Christian marriage, but the conventions of Courtly Love as well. Certainly this is true of the prepotent Satyr-*homme sauvage,* whom Spenser portrayed in Book III of his *Faerie Queene* (written not long before Shakespeare invented Caliban) proving his powers with the faithless Hellenore, as her betrayed husband looks on: "Who all night long did mind his joyous play: Nine times he heard him come aloft ere day. . . ." Interestingly enough, America is much on Spenser's mind in this very book; elsewhere in the forest Belphoebe (intended, perhaps, to suggest Elizabeth the Queen) is tending the wounds of Timias (surely modeled on Sir Walter Raleigh) with "divine tobacco."

But the association of the Satyrs with the Western world is older far than Jacobean or even Elizabethan times. In Pausanias' *History of Greece,* the author explains that "wishing to know better than most people who the Satyrs are," he had gone about inquiring, and had heard of a certain Euphemus the Carian, who

> was driven out of his course by winds and was carried into the Outer Sea, beyond the course of seamen. He affirmed that there were many uninhabited islands, while in others lived wild men. . . . The islands were called the Satyrides by the sailors, and the inhabitants were red haired, and had upon their flanks tails not much smaller than those of horses. As soon as they caught sight of their visitors, they ran down to the ship without uttering a cry and assaulted the women in the ship. At last the sailors in fear cast a foreign woman on to the island. Her the Satyrs outraged not only in the usual way, but also in a most shocking manner.

One modern commentator on this strange passage is driven to speculate about whether the inhabitants of the Satyrides may not have been the infamous Caribs themselves, who, he assures us, were in the habit of "putting on horses' tails, smearing their heads red, and behaving nastily."

While this identification may strike us as highly improbable, Shakespeare at least had no trouble transferring to his Carib-Cannibal-Caliban the sexuality long attributed to defunct myths: the longing to deflower and violate rather than worship and woo woman.

In fact, the natives of America did not practice rape generally until they learned it from their European invaders, and then they could achieve it only under the influence of the White Man's alcohol. They were, indeed, so continent sexually, so accustomed to long periods of enforced chastity while hunting or making war, that the French proto-anthropologists of the seventeenth century decided the Indians must be demi-eunuchs, hermaphroditic at least. But Shakespeare was no anthropologist; his small firsthand knowledge of Indians came from the few he saw exhibited as freaks or read about in broadsides, including one with a giant phallus to whom he refers during a mob scene in *Henry VIII*: "Or have we some Indian with the great tool come to court, the women so besiege us? Bless me, what a fry of fornication is at the door!"

It is with fornication, at any rate, that he associates Caliban, whose claims against Prospero, both spoken ("You stole my land!") and unspoken ("You'd never have let me marry your daughter!"), he permits the latter to answer with the countercharge:

> . . . I have us'd thee,
> (Filth as thou art) with humane care, and lodg'd thee
> In mine own cell till thou didst seek to violate
> The Honour of my child.

To which Caliban, his lust aroused (and with it, his desire to prove himself fully human by impregnating the daughter of his expropriator), is made to answer:

> O ho, O ho! would't had been done!
> Thou didst prevent me; I had peopled else
> The isle with Calibans.

And it is for this—for his unredeemed carnality and the vaunt of equality implicit in it, since only those of a single species can mate and reproduce—that Caliban is not merely nominated in the *dramatis personae "a savage and deformed slave,"* but demonstrated in the action to be self-condemned to remain so, because determined, unless restrained by force, to turn the whole White world Caliban, which is to say, half-breed.

The alternative to Montaigne's cultural relativism, which defines the Indian as one more acceptable breed of man, is Shakespeare's racism, which treats him as a demibeast, a domestic animal—unless, improbably, he attain grace. Preparing to exit, Caliban says:

> I'll be wise hereafter
> And seek for grace. What a thrice-double ass
> Was I, to take this drunkard for a god . . .

But Prospero's curt dismissal ("Go to! Away!") suggests that the Monster cannot long refrain from self-destructive idolatry. Shakespeare is, that is to say, not the sort of racist to whom non-Whites represent lower stages on the evolutionary scale, but a Christian one, to whom the American savage in his unredeemed world seemed the child of the forces of darkness, begotten by a demon on a witch, "hag-seed," a "demi-devil."

Montaigne avoids this judgment by retreating to the fable of Atlantis and the notion of a multiple creation, many races in many worlds. For Shakespeare, however, in this most orthodox of plays, there is no way out. "A devil, a born devil, on whose nature nurture can never stick!" cries Prospero of Caliban, speaking surely for the author of them both. And Miranda, in a speech so harshly unremitting that the editors keep trying to take it away from her, makes clear the ethnic source of her contempt:

> But thy vile race,
> Though thou didst learn, had that in't which
>   good natures
> Could not abide to be with.

No wonder, then, that the Utopian vision of a second chance at an Earthly Paradise (a Paradise never really lost but only for a time concealed), the benign secularization of Dante's doctrinal nightmare, which moved Montaigne to such eloquence, is rendered by Shakespeare as the unworldly maunderings of Gonzalo, an old man, virtuous, perhaps, but incapable of learning from experience and impotent to influence any events for the better in any world, Old or New, at sea or on land. Inspired by the prospect of the island on which he has been wrecked, Gonzalo says:

> Had I the plantation of this isle, my lord . . .
> All things in common nature should produce
> Without sweat or endeavor. Treason, felony,
> Sword, pike, knife, gun, or need of any engine
> Would I not have; but nature should bring forth,
> Of its own kind, all foison, all abundance,
> To feed my innocent people.

But he is mocked, even as he dreams aloud, by his two quite un-innocent comrades: first by Sebastian ("No marrying among his subjects!"), then Antonio, who picks up the raillery of his associate in cynicism ("None, man! all idle —whores and knaves"). Like Shakespeare himself, they have sex on their minds, and therefore little hope.

And the events which follow further undercut Gonzalo's foolish boast: "I would with such perfection govern, Sir, t'excel the golden age." There were already cues in history for Shakespeare to follow: the first ill-fated experiment at colonizing Virginia, and the difficulties of Jamestown only three years after its founding; these cues, plus his poetic prescience, he used to create around Caliban a paradigm of the tragi-comedy of "plantation."

"The savage and deformed slave," who thinks of himself

as having been brutally expropriated, offends the master and young mistress who think they have been blessedly "civilizing" him—and is, consequently, treated like a beast of burden. But new masters, the scum of the Old World, offer themselves to him, promising him and themselves unaccustomed sovereignty in the New World, and with the aid of whiskey winning him to their side ("That's a brave god and bears celestial liquor. I will kneel to him. . . .").

Once he has paid his grotesque homage to them, the White renegades support the monster in his dream of a Slave's Revolt against the proper ruler of them all:

> , . . with a log
> Batter his skull, or paunch him with a stake,
> Or cut his wesand with a knife.

They respond especially to his hatred for the culture of books, which they, too, know is the source of the legitimate authority of the Master of Arts:

> Having first seized his books. . . . Remember
> First to possess his books; for without them
> He's but a sot. . . . Burn but his books.

And through it all ring the cadences of Caliban's song, not an actual transcript of Indian chants like those Montaigne reproduces, but a kind of native American poetry created in contempt of European letters:

> No more dams I'll make for fish,
>   Nor fetch in firing
>   At requiring,
> Nor scrape trenchering, nor wash dish.
>   'Ban, 'Ban, Ca—Caliban
>   Has a new master. Get a new man.
> Freedom, high-day! high-day freedom! freedom, high-day, freedom!

In the play, of course, Caliban and his *lumpen* allies are not permitted to succeed—though they do interrupt, and interrupting, impugn Prospero's own vision of a Christian Utopia in which not nature, but married chastity insures a miraculous fertility without destructive passion, a world of increase over which Juno and Ceres preside, but not their hot sister, Venus, or her "waspish-headed son."

"I had forget that foul conspiracy of the beast Caliban and his confederates. . . ." Prospero says in the midst of a masque enacted by the spirits at his command, and at his signal of distress, they "heavily vanish. . . ."

By that time, however, it is all there: the history of America, early and late, from the Indian Wars to the rise and fall of slavery; from the triumph of a democracy of fugitive slaves which so vexed D. H. Lawrence ("A vast republic of escaped slaves. Look out, America! And a minority of earnest, self-tortured people. The masterless. *Ca Ca Caliban/Get a new master, be a new man*") to the revolt against the alphabet of which Marshall McLuhan is the prophet.

But *The Tempest* is judgment as well as history in mythological form: it is Europe judging and rejecting not only that native American, the Indian, but all the White Americans to come, who will—inevitably—remake themselves in the Indian's image. Yet the rejection is not finally a total one; for at almost the last possible moment, the spokesman for European culture acknowledges that the "new man" born of the powers of darkness is somehow also engendered by him. How can he not confess, at the very verge of putting his magic powers aside and begging to be "reliev'd by prayer," that the attempted rape of the virginal daughter in her scholar-father's cell was his Old World nightmare before it became a New World fact? How appropriately the confession comes in the midst of those last plays, all haunted by the threat of father-daughter incest explicitly stated in *Pericles*; and how much more appropriately in an England just realizing that, whatever its imperfections, the Anglo-Saxon plantation of the West was there to stay.

". . . this thing of darkness," Prospero says, even as the great lottery for Jamestown is being held in the world outside the theater, "I acknowledge mine."

THE BASIC MYTHS, I: THE END OF PETTICOAT GOVERNMENT

THE WEST may have been, along with that first of Westerners, the Indian, an invention of Europe, a projection of its fears and hopes, as Prospero seems to declare. But once Europeans began to settle in the West they had long dreamed and to cohabit or battle with the Indians who were there waiting, the myths which they inherited were radically altered, becoming myths not of others but of themselves. To be sure, the "savage man of Inde" was still their center, since in our native mythology colored men (the Indian first of all—then, in his image, the rest as we encounter them) play the part played by gods and demons, gnomes and kobolds and elves in Old World fables; indeed, women seem the only other supernatural or transhuman creatures viable in archetypal American tales. Between them, at any rate, women and Indians make for us a second, home-grown definition of what we consider the Real West, the West of the West, as it were; a place to which White male Americans flee from their own women into the arms of Indian males, but which those White women, in their inexorable advance from coast to coast, destroy.

Four myths in their interweaving create this image of the Far West: one made in Virginia at the beginning of the seventeenth century, one in Massachusetts at the end; one in Montreal at the beginning of the nineteenth, and one in New York at its end. The first is *The Myth of Love in the Woods*, or the story of Pocahontas and Captain John Smith, which presumably occurred in 1607—before *The Tempest* was written and in the first difficult year of the Jamestown settlement—but which did not take on anything like its final form until Smith had redreamed his youthful adventure in neglect and poverty, eight years after the death of Shakespeare, seven years past the point where an indignant Pocahontas (renamed Rebecca, properly married, and presented at the Court of King James) could have risen up to give him the lie. Most Americans do not know the story, however, even in the version of 1624, but only as recast by the sentimental imagination of the early nineteenth century, to which period the myth, therefore, effectively belongs.

The second is *The Myth of the White Woman with a Tomahawk*, the account of Hannah Duston, a New England lady who, snatched out of childbed by an Indian raiding party, fought her bloody way to freedom. At first glance, this seems just another of those Indian Captivity chronicles, known to most readers in the free adaptations of James Fenimore Cooper, though usually represented in school anthologies by the insufferably dull and pious journal of Mrs. Mary Rowlandson. But Hannah Duston is really quite another matter, as writers like Cotton Mather, Nathaniel Hawthorne, and Henry David Thoreau—each of whom retold the story in his own way—seem later to have realized.

The third is *The Myth of the Good Companions in the Wilderness*, the story of a White Man and a Red who find solace and sustenance in each other's love, identified for most Americans with the encounter of Fenimore Cooper's Natty Bumppo and Chingachgook over the embers of a dying fire. In its aboriginal form, however, it dates back to the *Adventures* of the fur-trapper Alexander Henry, who memorialized, in his old age and in the midst of a thriving city, his companionship as a youth in the wilderness with the Indian Wawatam.

The fourth is *The Myth of the Runaway Male*, given its archetypal name and shape once and for all in 1819 (at the moment when the Pocahontas idyll was being redeemed for the female reader), in Washington Irving's "Rip Van Winkle": the tale of a man who deserted his wife for a twenty years' sleep and returned to find her (happily) dead.

It is well to be clear about what these four myths have in common, and especially about the fact that all four arise (as myths most often do) at the limits of the "human," i.e., on that mythological frontier which writers tend to identify with actual geographical frontiers, where men of a particular culture confront creatures of another, who challenge their definition of the human by living out possibilities which they themselves have rejected or not yet imagined. For the WASP male in America, the women he brings with him from the Old World seem to face him across such a Frontier, quite as much as the savages he meets in the New World; or more precisely, once transplanted he finds himself straddling a boundary between two regions, each a little alien to him, one inhabited by females and the other by Redskins: the Clearing, as we come to say, and the Wilderness. With what he perceives as he faces first one way and then the other, our four myths deal.

The Story of Pocahontas deals with the encounter of Red Woman and White Man, that of Hannah Duston with the conflict of White Woman and Red Man; the tale of Wawatam treats exclusively the confrontation of White Man and Red, that of Rip Van Winkle the conflict of Man and Woman.

Actually, Europeans had begun—as we have observed in Shakespeare and Montaigne—to create a mythology of Dark Men and Light. But there was in Europe a counter-mythology, which never took root in American soil, that inhibited the development of a full-fledged color mythology on the other side of the Atlantic. This was the mythology of Class, which survived the dissolution of a courtly society to determine the shape of the European novel as well as of European political thinking right up to our own day, creating the large social myths which have determined the social fate of the Old World, as well as the smaller literary ones which have transformed its books.

What is involved in the mythology of class is the projection by adherents to the Code of Honor of all which that

Code forbids them on to certain other members of their society—different not ethnically, but in training, garb, diet, speech, habits of lovemaking, etc. Such a mythology leads to the creation of characters like Sancho Panza and Leperello, privileged cowards and boors, who have no precise counterparts in our literature. Similarly, the comradeship of gentlemen and manservant is unheard of in classic American books, though in the English novel, for instance, it is standard from the *Pickwick Papers* to P. G. Wodehouse's stories about Jeeves and Bertie Wooster or, for that matter, J. R. R. Tolkien's *The Lord of the Rings*. Even *Robinson Crusoe*, otherwise so oddly like an American book, with its striking parallel to the myth of the Good Companions in the Wilderness, parts company with our own similar books at the point where Friday is taught "Master" as his first word.

In any case, what the gods stood for in Greek literature and devils in medieval legend, what servants symbolize in European novels, women and colored men represent in our great books. In *Love and Death in the American Novel*, I observe that the only real equivalent to the class struggle in American fiction is the Battle of the Sexes, but I have come since to understand that this is merely the comic version of the class struggle, as it were; race conflict constitutes the pathetic, or even tragic version.

Thus the story of Rip Van Winkle is only *half* a proper American myth, embodying as it does only the comic, which is to say, the sexual equivalent to class conflict. Moreover, it is the single instance among the basic four of a myth imported from the Old World into the New, a piece of cultural baggage carried along with the emigrés. (In this sense, it is more like the Faust legend, the archetypal story of selling one's soul to the Devil, so often present in our literature, highbrow and low, yet remaining somehow stubbornly, unredeemably foreign.)

And finally, the legend of Rip represents the unique case of a myth deliberately adapted to the native scene by a self-conscious American author after the nation already existed politically. The first American short story, we like to call it; and it is, in fact, *about* the period in which the United States is born, though we do not ordinarily remember this. Rip's long sleep spans not only the last years of his wife's life, but also the two decades which separate the reign of the last English George to reign over us from that of the first American George to replace him: an uneasy transitional period which, Irving suggests, he would as lief have slept out, too, along with his proxy, Rip.

Washington Irving, dreaming, as it were, for the first time in his Europe-oriented life a truly American dream, created the first truly American figure, the first truly American plot to pass into the public domain. By the same token, he had begun to invent the character of the White Westerner and the fable appropriate to Western fiction; but for a long time Rip was claimed by New Englanders, as if his mythic home were their inclement North, especially when the brief, late spring mitigated its rigors.

Oliver Wendell Holmes, for instance, revived him as Rip Van Winkle, M.D., to amuse a meeting of the Massachusetts Medical Society in 1870, evoking his irresponsible spirit in a poem that closed, "Rip! Rip Van Winkle! time for you to wake! Laylocks in blossom! 'Tis the Month of May!" And before Holmes's time, Herman Melville had called a short story "Rip Van Winkle's Lilac"—reimagining Rip as the prototype of the Bohemian artist who prefers the joyous shade of a lilac bush growing from the ruins of what was once his house and home to the shelter of the prim white church with its mournful copse of willows.

Nathaniel Hawthorne seems to have been even more possessed than Melville by the figure and fable of Rip; he tells in *The Wonder Book* of one who was tempted to rehearse the tale of the man "who slept away twenty years at a stretch," but who rejected that temptation finally because "the story had been told once already, and better than it could ever be told again. . . ." Nonetheless, Hawthorne kept flirting with another version in a proposed novel called *Agatha:* the most notable unwritten novel in our history, since Melville, too, thought for a while about trying his hand at it. *Agatha* would apparently have been a kind of Van-Winkelized *Enoch Arden* in a Northern setting: the account of a sailor who returns home after a long voyage (surely it would have lasted the mythological twenty years) to find his wife not dead, as in Irving, nor even remarried, as in Tennyson, but, alas, alive and waiting for him, so that he has to flee once more. But who can be Rip Van Winkle twice in a single lifetime? Hawthorne could neither manage to write it nor persuade Melville to try.

Instead, he produced the odd little story "Wakefield," the tale of a man who, as "a little joke . . . at his wife's expense," disappears for the legendary two decades. But when Wakefield comes back, he finds the same supremely unhappy ending that had wrecked *Agatha:* a wife still alive —though this time seen only from the street, a shadow on the blinds, laughing her last laugh. This is not at all the sort of last laugh that the authentic myth of Rip affords.

Most ambitious of all the latter-day exploiters of Rip, however, is Hart Crane, whose long poem *The Bridge* attempted a full-scale resumé of American mythology, from the viewpoint this time of a mid-Westerner, an inhabitant of that uneasy mid-region between Northeast and West. And in *The Bridge,* despite its obvious indebtedness to those "Eastern" writers, T. S. Eliot and Ezra Pound, the experiencing consciousness is no classical figure like the Tiresias of Eliot's *The Waste Land* or the Ulysses of Pound's *Cantos,* but Rip himself, which is to say, an American improbably seeking his West in the streets of New York.

> And Rip forgot the office hours,
>   and he forgot the pay;
> Van Winkle sweeps a tenement
>   way down on Avenue A. . . .

"And hurry along, Van Winkle—" the poet urges the archetype he evoked and could not control, at the end of the section called by his name, "it's getting late." But it is, of course, even later now, thirty-five years after Crane's death, *much* later; yet still that dim evasive figure moves with us out of our past toward whatever future lies ahead. Meaning what, we are driven to ask, generation after generation, signifying *what?*

The answer is not to be found, surely, in scrutinizing the ultimate origins of the Rip story, though some have tried that tack; patient scholars have uncovered for us the European source of Irving's tale in a German legend called "Peter Klaus the Goatherd." And Philip Young, in a rewarding though limited article in the *Kenyon Review*, traced the mythic materials of the European prototype back to sources even more remote. What is remarkable and significant, however, is not the European past, but the American future of the tale: the differences of Irving's version from its presumed original and the surmised antecedents of that.

It is Irving who invents the character of Rip's wife and his difficult relationship with her, Irving who first portrays Dame Van Winkle as an intolerably efficient and shrewish wife. "A termagant wife may . . ." he writes, "be considered a tolerable blessing; and if so, Rip Van Winkle was thrice blessed." The irony is obvious and easy enough; but just so simply he turns the old story of the Enchanted Sleeper (about whose wife no one could possibly care) into something new under the sun: a comic inversion of the legend of the Persecuted Maiden—a corresponding male fantasy of persecution, appropriate to a country that likes to think of itself, or endures being thought of, as the first matriarchy of the modern world.

There have been tales of long-term sleepers from the beginning of time: the Seven Sleepers, La Belle au Bois Dormante. But such traditional sleepers awakened to worlds of acceptance and love, not to old-age loneliness. Only in the American version is the happy ending determined by the death of a wife rather than the appearance of a lover. (Here, once and for all, is invented that oddly desolate American, that ultimately Western, denouement which so sharply distinguishes, say, the conclusion of *Huckleberry Finn* from that of *Oliver Twist*.)

Similarly, there have been men in myth and fable snatched out of the ordinary world across the borders of enchantment; but from Scotland to Japan, such men have been traditionally lured by beautiful uncanny females promising sexual pleasure beyond the scope of mere humans—surely not by a night of hard drinking with fellow males.

Some of this is already implicit in the German source, but it is Irving alone who fully realizes the importance to the Rip myth of drinking, the archetypal significance of gin ritually consumed with the boys as a protest against home and wife. So, also, it is Irving who creates the first drunk to come reeling through the pages of a native American work: the prototype of tens of thousands of fictional protagonists and almost as many American authors—re-embodied generation after generation in the partially mythologized lives as well as in the partially autobiographical characters even of quite recent writers like Scott Fitzgerald and Hemingway and Faulkner.

" 'Oh! that flagon! that wicked flagon!' thought Rip—'What excuse shall I make to Dame Van Winkle!' " And his cry has never ceased echoing in our heads.

If we have been in fact, in the United States, a self-declared and self-celebrated Whiskey Culture for a couple of centuries—if booze has been the not-so-secret weapon of the WASP male against his two transhuman mythological enemies, Indians and women—Irving deserves credit, along with Benjamin Franklin, for having been the first to perceive it. Between them, they tell the whole tale, Franklin observing of the Indians (with the bland assurance that so annoyed D. H. Lawrence), "And, indeed, if it be the design of Providence to extirpate these savages in order to make room for the cultivators of the earth, it seems not improbable that rum may be the appointed means. It has already annihilated all the tribes who formerly inhabited all the sea coast—"; and Irving not quite saying as much of women, but implying it in his archetypal tale. Wives were the only mythic subject on which he felt, at that point, moved to comment; about Indians, he seems to have known little and cared less—though later in life he was to turn to the American West in search of a subject to titillate an audience jaded with European scenes.

His earlier obtuseness about Indians is, in fact, one of the things which undercuts the final effectiveness of his myth, keeps it from playing as decisive a role in our psychic lives as the three others. But there are other factors which obviate its archetypal potency as well. His telling of the tale is, to begin with, disconcertingly comic in tone, undercut by the apologetic wit characteristic of overconscious mythmakers. All the most disturbing implications of Irving's tale, what it seems to *want* to mean despite him, are qualified by the irony proper to a demirebel who only playfully mocks the institutions he is afraid seriously to challenge. "I don't believe it," Irving's tone seems constantly to be saying, not only of the supernatural elements in his story, but also of his attack on woman and marriage.

There is, however, a persistent note of melancholy beneath the humor, the melancholy of one just a little sad that he is not just a little braver, but also the melancholy of one who, writing a fable of change, deliverance, revolution, knows all the time that *plus ça change, plus c'est la même chose.* On the level of politics, this aspect of Irving's tone suggests that the American Revolution may not have changed much by merely swapping one red-faced George for another. And in terms of domestic matters, it implies that even the "petticoat government," which Rip felt was "happily . . . at an end" when he descended from the hills (since his wife *was* dead, having burst a blood-vessel screaming at a Yankee peddler), still survived, though in another form. Looking about him in a presumably new world, Rip discovers almost immediately that his son has turned into the very image of himself, and is, presumably, ready to begin living all over again the pattern-story of henpeckery and evasion. And he recognizes his daughter first when she yells (quite in the voice of his late termagant wife) to a third-generation little Rip, "Hush, Rip . . . hush, you little fool . . ." It must have seemed an echo out of a past never quite dead enough.

But what makes the Rip myth finally eccentric—and just a little irrelevant—is Irving's failure to dream for Rip appropriate good companions to whom he can flee. Like Natty Bumppo a little later on, Rip is equipped with a gun and a dog; and like Natty, he seeks virgin land when he takes off from home, a stretch of undomesticated nature fit for a hunting man and his faithful hound. But Rip does not go far enough—only to the easy slopes of the Catskills, where he finds the ghosts of certain jolly old Dutchmen (for mythological reasons of his own, or merely playful ones, Irving turns the English Henry Hudson into a Dutch Hendrick), those comic Netherlandish wraiths who so possessed Irving's imagination, but who do not possess our own.

Dutchmen are too palefaced and civilized for the American mythological mind; and even a dog, though better by far than a European, will not do as a good companion. In a poem called "Benjamin Pantier," included in his *Spoon River Anthology*, Edgar Lee Masters attempts many years later to portray a kind of Rip who holes up in an abandoned office with a dog for his sole anti-wife; but even Masters makes a concession to the mythological necessities of the case by calling that dog "Nig." It is, however, *real* colored men that we want by the side of our runaway Whites, not beasts with metaphorical names—Indians, if possible, and Indians are just what Irving cannot quite give us in the year 1819, though they float about everywhere in his story, as if they were trying to break through despite the author's intentions.

Rip himself, we learn, has told the village children stories of "ghosts, witches, and Indians . . ." (two imported kinds of spook and one native one), while his daughter Judith is sure that he has been "carried away by Indians." Yet despite such hints and clues, Irving could evoke no actual Red Men in his potentially Western tale; and maybe, after all, it was the whiskey that got in his way, since the saloon and the forest seem to stand not merely for alternative, but mutually exclusive, anti-homes. In the former, the Indian is banned, being incapable of holding his liquor; while in the latter, he is a companion and guide *except* when drunk, for then he becomes a menace even to those he loves. For better or worse, at any rate, the American imagination has a hard time combining whiskey and Indians in any tale not conceived in disaster and written out of hate.

To satisfy our deep archetypal hunger, the Rip story has to be re-created, radically revised, the tone converted from irony to nostalgia, Wawatam substituted for Hendrick Hudson. Only then can the refugee male become the hero of us all: the model of all those anti-heroic heroes who continually extended the West, since they rebelled no more than they conformed, neither coming into their inheritances and settling down nor killing their fathers and challenging the power of the State, but instead going West, i.e., running away from home.

But westering, in America, means leaving the domain of the female, since in our classic books fathers are usually invisible or conveniently dead. Rip, despite his mythological shortcomings, is the first of those escapees from what women call responsibility, the first American character shiftless enough to be loved by the audience which loves Cooper's Natty Bumppo, Melville's Ishmael, and Mark Twain's Huck Finn, as well as Saul Bellow's Henderson the Rain King and the hero of Ken Kesey's *One Flew Over the Cuckoo's Nest*.

Precisely for this reason, women found Irving's fable of this escape and return too fundamentally anti-feminist to bear. But the satisfactions he denied them, certain dramatic reworkings of his story in the later nineteenth century provided in overflowing measure. Women, who went to the theater in those days to learn to love themselves and to bemoan their plight, could scarcely fault the Van Winkle plays that held the stage for half a century or more—especially those in which the title role was played by Joseph Jefferson III.

Jefferson, last of a long line of popular actors of the same name, was also a playwright of sorts, who combined and revised earlier dramatic versions of the tale by Thomas Flynn, John Kerr, and Charles Burke, creating at last the form of the Rip story in which the largest public was to know it for many years. He had made his debut in a minstrel show, a decade or so after the publication of Irving's Rip, as a small boy in black face, dumped out of a sack by Thomas D. Rice, inventor of the famed Jim Crow routine; but it was as the runaway White rather than the comic Nigger that he was long remembered.

As early as 1850, he had worked out the renowned characterization which he continued to play until 1904, how many times in all it would be hard to say. By 1881, at any rate, he was writing, "I think I have played 'Rip Van Winkle' about 2500 times—and for which I may be forgiven in another and better world where there will be no matinees and no managers." But what a strangely transformed Rip he enacted: a myth debased and sentimentalized, an archetype turned stereotype. He complicated Irving's simple plot by the addition of a cruel landlord threatening that foreclosure of the mortgage so inevitable in nineteenth century plays, and by the build-up of Rip's daughter, renamed for some inscrutable reason "Meenie" and endowed with two rival suitors, one as admirable as the other was detestable.

Most disconcertingly of all, however, Rip's wife is married off, after his disappearance, to a second husband, the avaricious holder of the mortgage, whose bullying makes her aware of the despised virtues of her first and converts her from a shrew into a model wife. Even before Rip's departure out into the required raging storm, the pathos begins to build. "Why, Gretchen," he cries to his wife, "are you going to turn me out like a dog?" And little Meenie, his tearful daughter, pleads, "No father, don't go," even as Rip murmurs in response, "My child! Bless you, my child, bless you!" after which, the stage directions inform us, "Meenie faints," and "Rip gives a sobbing sigh." For one moment, even the harsh wife relents, and calls out, "No, Rip! Husband come back!" But it is too late; offended and a man at last, he leaves all the same. And this time, we are told, "Gretchen faints," leaving the stage with two unconscious female forms, and, presumably, no dry eye in the house.

After a twenty-year lapse of time, Rip, returning from his long sleep, discovers Dame Van Winkle still very much alive, but sufficiently chastened to cry out, "Oh, Rip! I drove you from home; but do not desert me again. I'll never speak an unkind word to you, and you shall never see a frown on my face. And Rip . . . You may stay out all night, if you like . . . And, Rip, you can get tight as often as you please." After this, there is nothing left for Rip to do but toss off a drink with a wink and a grin, as the curtain descends; and, leaving the darkened house, husbands join with their wives in the pretense that just such a reconciliation is what they have both wanted all along—what, in fact, they have achieved in their own homes. Like all stereotypes, Jefferson's *Rip Van Winkle* tells a comforting lie in place of a disheartening truth, and like many of them, was clearly doomed from the start to success.

THE BASIC MYTHS, II:
LOVE IN THE WOODS

JOE JEFFERSON's Rip may have achieved on the popular stage a reconciliation with his wife, miraculously preserved for him, to please the ladies. But such an ending satisfies the deep American imagination even less than the encounter with European ghosts in a native landscape, which Irving proposed in its stead. It is an Indian Rip must embrace—a male if possible, but in any case some dusky non-European; and this Hart Crane seems to have understood when he sat down to write *The Bridge*, though his own homosexuality—in a decade which still demanded reticence in such matters—apparently got in his way.

The Bridge is doomed from the start, though, not only by its author's sexual problems, but by its ill-fated resolve to weave together the two most readily debased tales in our archetypal heritage with a third, more stereotype than myth from the moment of its conception.

> There was Priscilla's cheek close in the wind
> And Captain Smith, all beard and certainty,
> And Rip Van Winkle, bowing by the way . . .

Crane writes in the section of his intended epic called by Van Winkle's name. And though we hear no more of the insufferable Priscilla (whose vicarious wooing by Miles Standish had long since been made into a classroom bore by Longfellow), Captain Smith, it turns out, has entered Crane's imagination long enough at least to leave there forever his legendary companion in the Virginia woods,

Pocahontas: "the mythological nature-symbol," Crane calls her in a letter to his patron, Otto Kahn, "chosen to represent the physical body of the continent or the soil."

By the time Crane got round to taking her up, however, Pocahontas had become as much a staple of sentimental ladies' literature as Longfellow's poor Priscilla. Yet he apparently believed that she was what Rip had been trying to dream, in secret from his original author and those who dramatized him, all century long: apt symbol of the White man's reconciliation with our land and its first inhabitants. Or at least this is what Crane would deceive us (and/or himself) into believing. But *why*, we are driven to ask. What led him—aside from the fact that formally he was uneducated and therefore the victim of his mother's and his grade school teachers' taste—to so ill-fated a choice?

The Pocahontas legend, despite its connection with the first American West, is one which left untouched the imagination of our classic writers; it moved chiefly the producers of popular entertainment in prose and verse, between covers and on the stage, from the close of the eighteenth century to the verge of our own time. Plays, as we have already noticed in the case of Rip, were the chief carriers of our earliest pop culture; and scores of Pocahontas plays were, in fact, written, though not one of real merit. Nonetheless, ever since the stage success of James Nelson Barker's *The Indian Princess, or La Belle Sauvage*, large numbers of playwrights have been tempted to explore the dramatic possibilities of the subject, right down to Vergil Geddes' *Pocahontas and the Elders*. Even the step-grandson of George Washington—that George Washington Parke Custis who used to deliver a Fourth of July oration each year dressed in a Roman toga, and who lived long enough to become the father-in-law of General Robert E. Lee—produced a version; this is surely as honorable an ancestry as an American play can have.

If Pocahontas became somehow a symbol of patriotic pride to all Americans, as well as our first mythic Indian and a subject of sentimental interest to women, it is perhaps because, at the very moment she was being kidnapped by the ladies' writers, her figure was being blended into that of the "Indian Princess," as the title of Barker's play indicates. The Indian Princess was, as few realize in the age of Uncle Sam, the first symbol of the United States, representing the Western wilderness reclaimed by civilization. E. McClung Fleming of the Winterthur Museum, who has closely studied her iconography, describes the Princess much as we imagine Pocahontas herself:

> The Indian Princess was usually portrayed as a handsome, vigorous, Indian woman in her twenties. She is of noble visage and bearing, has a swarthy complexion and long, dark hair, wears a feathered headdress and skirt or cape and is usually uncovered to the waist. She is customarily armed with a bow and a quiver of arrows. . . .

And he goes on to speculate about her relationship to the earlier icon of the Indian Queen, the true *Belle Sauvage*, who first stood for the newly discovered West:

> . . . the Indian Princess as a symbol of the American colonies of Great Britain was in part derived from the Indian Queen familiar to Europeans for two hundred years as a symbol of the Western hemisphere. It was Martin Waldseemuller's *Cosmographie Introductio* of 1507 that first gave the name "America" to the New World, and that first suggested that this new world was a fourth continent or fourth part of the world supplementing Asia, Africa and Europe. . . .

We are back on familiar ground again, at the moment when the tripartite world is about to acknowledge its long forbidden fourth direction and, as we might expect, the "Caribs" are waiting to greet us once more. Mr. Fleming continues:

> Since each of the three older continents had for many years been symbolized in the arts by a queenly figure

representing the characteristic face of that continent, the European imagination now immediately set to work evolving a symbol of this new world. Quite naturally the new figure was based on the notions that had become current, with the publication of the first travel accounts of America, of the appearance, habits, and surroundings of the barbarous Indians of the semi-tropical Caribbean region. . . .

The Indian Queen is, in short, a sister to—or perhaps better, the mother of—Carib-Cannibal-Caliban:

. . . the Queen usually was depicted, in visage, as having a swarthy or "tawney" hue; in size, as being Amazonian; in dress, as wearing a feathered headdress and feathered skirt sometimes supplemented by a feathered cape and jewelled anklets . . . the Queen was armed with a club. . . . A particularly barbarous touch was the bloody, severed head of a man pierced by an arrow and lying near the feet of the Queen. . . .

Though Mr. Fleming does not say so explicitly, it is clear by implication that the Indian Princess is derived from the Indian Queen by turning a full-blown dangerous mother into a virginal protective daughter, slimming her down and reducing her in size from a giant to a girl, underplaying her sexuality and brutality alike, taking the club from her hand and giving it to her off-stage brother-father, which is to say, Caliban. She becomes, in short, a kind of dusky woodland Diana, a "huntress chaste and fair," who, quite soon, is blanched out into those somewhat later palefaced female symbols of the United States: the Neo-Classical Goddess, the American Liberty and Columbia. She keeps her feathers for a while, but instead of a beast couched at her feet or a severed head, she has hogsheads of tobacco—to signify, perhaps, the process by which the natural fertility of the New World has been converted into Yankee dollars. But after a while, even her native headdress is taken from her and bestowed on a new colored import: a little Black slave, doubly exotic in his Red warrior's plumage. Just one of the girls at last, she is ready to have her portrait appear on a dime.

Meanwhile, as Pocahontas, she has lived a thousand lives in sentimental novels and semi-fictional biographies about which the less said the better, though anyone interested can find a first-rate bibliography, interwoven with critical commentary, in Philip Young's article called "The Mother of Us All" in the *Kenyon Review* of Summer, 1962. The poems inspired by her mythical connection with John Smith are even more banal—the best of a poor lot being, perhaps, one by George P. Morris, better known as the author of the equally execrable "Woodman, Spare that Tree." Morris's Pocahontas poem is one of four on the subject included in a collection of American popular songs edited by a certain William McCarty in 1842.

All four are reprinted—as they properly should be, considering the Indian maiden's symbolic identity with our nation itself—under the heading of "Patriotic Songs," side by side with such old-time favorites as "Hail Columbia!" "Above his head in air," Mr. Morris's verses begin as they reach the climactic scene, "the savage war-club swung." It is the image which thrills us especially: the stone axe in the hand of the threatening father, which never quite falls, as the White head of our hero is cradled in the dusky arms of the beautiful Indian lass.

> Above his head in air
>   The savage war-club swung:
> The frantic girl, in wild despair
>   Her arms about him flung.
> Then shook the warriors of the shade
>   Like leaves on aspen limb,
> Subdued by the heroic maid
>   Who breathed a prayer for him!

> "Unbind him!" gasp'd the chief;
> "It is your King's decree!"
> He kissed away the tears of grief,
> And set the captive free!
> 'Tis ever thus, when in life's storm
> Hope's star to man grows dim,
> An angel kneels, in woman's form,
> And breathes a prayer for him.

Reading these lines, we can see how utterly the male fantasies of Captain John Smith, exploited by the "planters" of the New World, were adapted in the nineteenth century to the Sentimental Love Religion whose secret scriptures are Samuel Richardson's best-selling novels, *Pamela* and *Clarissa,* and whose chief dogma is that not Jesus Christ but a Good Woman is the savior of sinful man. In Barker's play, too, the transformation has been made, Smith crying out, just after his rescue and presumable conversion to the underground religion of bourgeois ladies:

> Oh Woman! Angel Sex! where'er thou art,
> Still art thou heavenly. The rudest clime
> Robs not thy glowing bosom of its nature.

For Smith himself, however, the meanings of his supposed encounter with Pocahontas—dreamed seventeen years after the supposed fact—were quite other. He saw himself not as the beneficiary of the "Angel Sex," but as a beloved Paleface son-lover, always threatened by some dark-skinned husband-father, and always delivered in the nick of time by the daughter-wife of his adversary, won over by his charms.

The later sentimentalizers of the tale tended to make the Indian Maiden a little lighter in color than her evil papa, and, therefore, archetypally a little better; though, of course, she has to be somewhat darker than the White captive to keep the interracial flavor of the plot. In Joseph Croswell's play *A New World Planted*, for instance, one character remarks of an Indian girl here called "Pocahonta" and transplanted to New England: "I know she's browner than European dames, but whiter far, than other natives are."

To Smith it made no difference, dusky or quite dark, so long as the girl who crossed ethnic lines for his sake was something other than White. Actually he tells the archetypal story twice, setting it once in Turkey, once in Virginia. In the Turkish version, he portrays his assailant and protector as husband and wife, revealing the conventional Mediterranean Courtly Love Triangle behind the myth; in the American one, he makes them father and daughter, struggling for the life of one who, after the happy event, will be adopted by his erstwhile enemy as a son. And this constitutes not only a peculiarly Romantic version of the underlying Oedipal triangle, but an especially American one as well: one version of the reconciliation of White Man and Red in the wilderness.

To be sure, long before America and Romanticism, the ancient archetype of Oedipus had been adapted to the needs of the Christian imagination in the Legend of the Turk's Daughter, which portrays Jocasta—turned from mother to daughter, to begin with—as the offspring of an infidel wooed by a true believer. This Philip Young duly notes, without pausing to reflect, however, that even closer to the Idyll of Pocahontas is a variant of the type, best known to us from Shakespeare's *Merchant of Venice* and Sir Walter Scott's *Ivanhoe:* the Tale of the Jew's Absconding Daughter.

Not Scott nor even Shakespeare, however, are its ultimate sources, but the Old Testament and the New, since it reflects the primitive terror of the Christian before the figure of Abraham, that archetypal Jewish Father with a Knife, set off against his love for the Virgin Mary, that archetypal Jewish Daughter. The Puritanism of the first Americans may have cut the rest of us off from any organized worship of the Blessed Virgin; but deep within us has survived an archetypal willingness to hate the alien father and love the alien daughter—whether these be Powhatan or Abraham, Pocahontas or the Mother of Christ. And, anyhow, for us,

Jew and Indian tend to fall together in the world of myth.

In Smith's *Generall Historie*, just as in *The Merchant of Venice*, the romantic subplot ends with the conversion of a Dusky Girl to Christianity and her marriage not to the hero himself (apparently the incest taboo operates here on some obscure but influential level), but to a friend of his, a convenient splitting off from the beloved son-brother. Smith, at least, unlike Shakespeare, could plead that history limited his fantasy; that, after all, Pocahontas had married John Rolfe in fact, before she saved his life in fiction.

How hard it is, however, for the child's mind, which loves the story of Pocahontas best of all, to remember, or, remembering, quite to believe that she married the *wrong* man. What it prefers to recall instead is her other mythological exploit—her slipping through the night, after her conversion, to warn her White lover's community of an impending attack by her father's people. Our first celebrated traitor to her own race is not merely a home-grown version of Shylock's daughter, but a model long in advance for Uncle Tom. Our first Tom is an Indian girl; and this, in our deepest national memory, we do not forget!

But there are troublesome ambiguities even here; for it was a *White* community which the Red Girl, Pocahontas, warned—just as it was a *White* man she married, and, before that, a *White* man she saved from death. Try, therefore, as they will, the sentimental writers for women cannot make her story a myth of Richardsonian salvation alone. It remains also, what Smith had dreamed it, a myth of reconciliation between the races by love and marriage. Any combination of sex and race raises for White Americans the bugaboo of miscegenation, so terrifyingly versified by Shakespeare, while Smith still trod the forests of Virginia in search of love.

Moreover, that demidevil, the Indian, is too closely associated in the WASP mind with the notion of rampant concupiscence to make possible a really viable synthesis of Pamela and Pocahontas; and anyhow, the Pure Young Girl of Anglo-Saxon mythology is typically blue-eyed and blonde, the proper color scheme for angels. Archetypally, Indian girls (like Italians or Jews or Moors) are assimilated to the image of the Dark Lady, symbol of passion which destroys as opposed to chastity which saves.

Historically, too, there is little to sustain the Pocahontas legend, since the typical relationship of White settlers to the Indian women they encountered was casual intercourse or long-term cohabitation without benefit of conversion or marriage. Completely aware of this, John Rolfe felt obliged to protest the purity of his own motives in marrying Pocahontas in a long letter to an influential friend, one paragraph of which runs as follows:

> Let therefore this my well advised protestation, which here I make betweene God and my own conscience, be a sufficient witnesse, at the dreadful day of judgement (when the secret of all mens harts shall be opened) to condemne me herein, if my chiefest intent and purpose be not, to strive with all my power of body and minde, in the undertaking of so mightie a matter, no way led (so farre forth as mans weaknesse may permit) with the unbridled desire of carnal affection: but for the good of this plantation, for the honour of our countrie, for the glory of God, for my owne salvation, and for the converting to the true knowledge of God and Jesus Christ an unbeleeving creature, namely Pokahuntas.

Even John Smith, outside of the few pages that the bourgeois-sentimental imagination seized on and expurgated, treats Pocahontas more cynically than romantically. He does not give us quite so irreverent a view of her as does his contemporary, William Strachey, who also knew her from childhood on (". . . a well-featured but wanton young girle, Powhatan's daughter . . . would get the boyes forth with her into the markett place, falling on their hands, turning their heeles upwards, whom she would followe and wheele so herselfe, naked as she was, all the fort over"), but he does remark coldly in one place, "She would have done what he listed."

And in another, he describes how she and her women came "naked out of the woods . . . singing and dancing . . . hanging about him, most tediously crying *Love you me not.*" (The "him" is, of course, Smith, who—like Caesar—refers to himself always in the third person.) "Naked" is the key word in this other, more frankly erotic vision of Pocahontas, which corresponds more closely to the sniggering attitude toward "squaws" that has persisted into our own time, and which helps explain why in our West the term "Princess" remains still a jocular name for the Indian prostitute.

Despite all this, the angelification of the Indian female has been tried over and over again in the United States for a host of local Red Wings, Minne-ha-ha's etc.; all of whom have passed rapidly into the realm of parody and burlesque. Kids still sing with some sense of blasphemy:

> There once was an Indian maid,
> Who always was afraid
> That some buckaroo
> Would slip it up her coo
> As she was gently sleeping in the shade. . . .

Indian maids have continued to be celebrated, all the same, in Chamber of Commerce handouts to tourists and round-the-Council-Fire sessions at Girl Scout Camps. A major attempt of this kind is represented by the legend of the young Snake woman, Sacajawea, or Sacagawea, a name which Meriwether Lewis—for whom the girl acted as guide and interpreter—understood to mean "Bird Woman," though the scholars now assure us its true, though homelier, significance is "Canoe Launcher."

To Lewis, who, along with William Clark and a tiny band of woodsmen, opened up the Far West, she was an object of no romantic interest; ". . . if she has enough to eat," he observes of her coolly at one point, "and a few trinkets to wear I believe she would be perfectly content anywhere."

He seems to have had no real affinity for women, to begin with, this protegé of Thomas Jefferson who was to die single; and what feeling he felt obliged by the conventions of his time to pretend toward "the Sex" he saved for White ladies back home, like that "Miss Maria W——d" who later married someone else, of course, but after whom he named a wilderness river, noting in his journal, "It is true that the hue of the waters of this turbulent and troubled stream but illy comport with the pure celestial virtues and amiable qualifications of that lovely fair one; but on the other hand it is a noble river. . . ."

With Indians, he was always the scientist, the field representative of the American Philosophical Society, more of a detached anthropologist than Montaigne himself. To be sure, he tended the "squar," as he generally called her, with the same care he bestowed on the other members of the expedition, including Clark's Negro slave, York, and his own dog: giving her ground snake rattles for birth pangs, when she bore a son on the trail; dosing her with "cataplasms of bark and laudanum" when she suffered severe menstrual pains. But all the while he observed her with an eye as dispassionate as the one he turned on the six whores an Indian madame brought to greet him when he reached the Pacific, or on the women of the Assiniboines, of whose grass girdles he observed in his notes:

> [They are] of a sufficient thickness when the female stands erect to conceal those parts usually covered from familiar view, but when she stoops or places herself in many other attitudes this battery of Venus is not altogether impervious to the inquisitive and penetrating eye of the amorite.

Nonetheless, Sacajawea has been mythicized and sentimentalized ever since, her name bestowed not only on a river, a mountain, and a pass, but on innumerable motels and grimy small-town cafés throughout the Mountain West. For better or for worse, this third wife of the French-Canadian Charbonneau (already betrothed to one Indian before her kidnapping and sale to him and destined to marry a couple more before she was through) has been transformed into a trans-Mississippi Pocahontas—which means that the popular mind has felt obliged to weave around her the story of an unconsummated love for the Great White Captain, as well as an account of her as an "Uncle Tom," apologist for her people's conquerors and mediator of their surrender.

In 1942, the popular legends about Sacajawea were gathered and rendered in a version perhaps intended for young adolescents by Donald Culross Peattie, who boasted in a foreword that "Whatever he has recounted here that is not stated in the records he believes can be discovered there between the lines." Nonetheless, we realize quite soon that the Indian girl he extrapolates from the scant lines Lewis and Clark gave her is more closely related to the Pocahontas dream than to the historical facts of the case: "he saw the intelligence, wary and tiptoe, moving behind the dark scorn in her stare. He saw how sturdily the little bronze body was made, and the face was lovely. . . . Sacajawea . . . was woman, essential, natural woman. She was innocent, ignorant of conscious charm. . . . Her dark eyes glittered like the night sky. . . . She was mysterious. . . ."

So much for the mythological New Pocahontas; and now for the mythological new Smith, the melancholy Lewis, dead by his own hand (or perhaps murdered at a point when he no longer had anything to live for) at the age of thirty-five: "Here we have him, the eternal, unresting pathfinder. . . . Men like that are the men who have got us as far as we are in civilization; only they can get us the rest of the way."

Given so stereotypical a pair, what follows for Peattie must be stereotype, too: "And beside a man like that, you may always look for a woman. . . . Uniquely the woman beside Meriwether Lewis . . . was not even of his color. They could not so much as talk together in one tongue. But they lived for one purpose, since her purpose was only his . . . it was a love as pure and clear and cold as the sources of the Missouri and Columbia. And out of it has descended to us as mighty a flow." But even this is not enough for Peattie, as it is not enough for the legend; Pocahontas is obliged not merely to kneel in angel form for her White master, but also to turn against her people for his sake:

> White men, beware!—and when, at last,
> Your fears are dead, and your dangers past,
> Shall the voice of the warner be e'er betray'd?
> Shall white men forget the Indian maid?

So also Peattie's Sacajawea is permitted to live on, long after the members of the expedition had thought her dead, to the age of nearly one hundred (as there is some evidence she may have), wearing not only her original name, and "Janey," the nickname Clark gave her, but others as well on her long way: "Lost Woman," "Constant Lover," "Porivo" (which means "Chief"), "Went-a-Long-Way."

And at the end of her trail, he portrays her, an old, old woman, pleading with her people to believe yet one more White lie, to accept yet one more retreat: ". . . Listen instead to the White men. I have known them long and long. Theirs is the great nation, the greatest. It marches always forward, in ways of peace and plenty. I have seen this. Now I have spoken." At which point, Pocahontas-Sacajawea becomes one with the old, old Indians of Fenimore Cooper (though his are always men), those ancients prophesying, welcoming, wishing their own doom, the disappearance of their people—becomes, in short, the Vanishing American.

The image of the Vanishing American, however, has possessed not only Fenimore Cooper and the popular mythicizers of Sacajawea. It has haunted all Americans, in their dreams at least if not in their waking consciousness; for it is rooted in our profoundest guilt: our awareness that we began our national life by killing something vital to the New World as well as something essential to the Old; by making an end of what had up until then been America, as well as what at that point was still Europe. The America which the first men to call themselves "Americans" destroyed (having to invent even a name for a place which had remained nameless as well as historyless) was the anonymous New World which had existed invisibly—unchanged and, as it were, unchangeable—outside the range of Europe for millenia, except of course for the incursions of dreams, which alone among the modes of exploration change nothing. If in relationship to the Old World, those first Americans were patricides, regicides, in the last analysis, deicides, in their relationship to the new, they were genocides, destroying the original inhabitants of the land they took for their own, the Indians.

Not quite destroying, really, for the act of genocide with which our nation began was inconclusive, imperfect, inhibited by a bad conscience, undercut by uncertainty of purpose. "There's no good injun but a dead injun," the really principled killers, which is to say, the soldiers, cried; but, "The next best thing is a Christian Indian," the soft-hearted castrators, which is to say, the Priests, reminded them; and, "We can get along with *any* Indian, so long as he's on a Reservation," the practical-minded ghetto-izers, which is to say, the bureaucrats and social workers, advised them both—having the final say. And so some Indians have survived among us: emasculated Indians, White Indians, Indians drunken and desolate and entrapped, knifing each other in sullen resentment, or piously praying in Baptist pews. For a while the nightmare of an End to their End, a resurrection of Indian power through Red Rebellion and Massacre continued to haunt us; but finally even that ceased to operate, as Custer's Last Stand became only a picture on a courthouse wall: a memorial not to Custer, whom a thousand repressive Custers succeeded, but to Sitting Bull, who proved the last of his threatening line. What continues to live on in our minds, what *we* continue to live and relive on the screens of movie houses and T.V. sets, on the pages of pulp magazines and paperback books, is the Legend of *their* End, which somehow (identifying in the darkened theatre or the living room with the lonely rider on the sage-brush-topped hill) we manage to feel as our End, since we share a single name with our conquered enemy: the Legend of the Vanishing American.

It is all there in that best-selling poem of the mid-nineteenth century, once memorized in huge chunks and gobbets by almost every American that went to grade school, then parodied and mocked by the children of such Americans, at last almost forgotten by their grandchildren, except as the dim reminiscence of an old joke. That best-seller is, of course, Longfellow's *Song of Hiawatha,* that intended epic, whose failed grandeur and comic badness we forget at considerable risk to ourselves, since bad poems tell a special kind of truth about the past which we cannot do without. A nation which expurgates from its anthologies those great bad poems it has loved, quite like a nation which refuses to include in those anthologies its great good ones, is a nation with only half a memory. Certainly *Hiawatha* catches in its genteel cadences, its academic sham of the primitive (the year of its publication, 1855, was—we remember—a great year for primitivism, seeing also the first edition of Whitman's *Leaves of Grass*) the sense of the End of the Original America, as revised and sentimentalized for a bourgeois reading public, who needed desperately to be reassured that if not all Indians, certain *better* Indians, at least, had welcomed the end of their, alas, pagan, though idyllic world.

The final section of Longfellow's poem opens, in any case, with the coming of the Christian missionaries to the shores of Gitchi Gumee:

> Came the Black-Robe Chief, the Prophet,
> He the Priest of Prayer, the Pale-face . . .

And the Black-Robe Chief loses little time in informing the circle of Redskin listeners, gravely puffing their pipes, not only

> . . . of the Virgin Mary
> And her blessed Son, the Saviour

but also of

> How the Jews, the tribe accursed,
> Mocked him, scourged him, crucified him . . .

Whereupon Hiawatha, until then sole teacher and leader of his people, decides that his day is over, and, lest *his* tribe prove as accursed as the perfidious Jews, delivers a valedictory warning:

> "I am going, O my people,
> On a long and distant journey . . .
> But my guests I leave behind me;
> Listen to their words of wisdom,
> Listen to the truth they tell you,
> For the Master of Life has sent them,
> From the land of light and morning!"

And in the closing lines of the poem, Longfellow reveals where his displaced Indian Culture Hero is tending:

> To the regions of the home-wind,
> Of the Northwest wind Keewaydin,
> To the Islands of the Blessed,
> To the Kingdom of Ponemah,
> To the land of the Hereafter!

But this ultimate West is, of course, the real America, which exists always beyond any historical America even as it existed before it: the America of the European dreamers, which departed the shores of our actual continent, once those self-styled bearers of truth and light had brought to it deceit and darkness—along with the possibility of verses like Longfellow's, more faithful to the wish than to the fact.

Not only in the United States, but on its border as well, the legend of the redemptive Indian girl has been adapted to local conditions and to other myths already shared by the peoples involved. Both Pocahontas and Sacajawea are, of course, Protestant versions of the encounter with the Indian, WASP fantasies of reconciliation in the wilderness.

When French Catholic Canada dreams an analogous dream, the differences are as illuminating as the resemblances. Its Pocahontas is the pious Mohawk maiden Catherine Tekakwitha, who was born in 1656 and died in 1680, still a virgin for the sake of Christ and the victim of her own ascetic practices, self-disciplined, self-tortured, self-immolated; she had fasted, had beat herself until the blood came, had slept night after night in a blanket pricked by hundreds of thorns; and, at last, on that Holy Wednesday, speech had failed her as she mumbled the names of Jesus and Mary. A little later she was dead, and a few moments afterward, the French priest praying beside her cried out in astonishment because her face had turned White. White—the complete conversion. No wonder she is proposed year after year for sainthood by believing *Canadiens* and *Canadiennes;* no wonder she is already worshipped as a saint by the more simple.

By what different means the French Catholic mind imagines the Indian girl making it, healing the intolerable breach between races; not by marriage and a court reception before the King in proper European dress, like Pocahontas-Rebecca Rolfe, but by virginity and a miraculous bleaching ("Though your sins be as scarlet—they shall be as white as snow").

And there is a third possibility still—another Roman Catholic alternative to the Indian as Protestant Angel—this time Latin-American. Representative of this solution is the mistress of Cortez, or more precisely the most famous of the mistresses of Cortez: an Indian girl, first called Malintzin, then renamed Marina after her baptism, the *"celèbre Mexicaine . . . belle comme une déesse. . . ."* So, at any rate, she is described in the *Grande Encyclopédie,* which goes on to say that, after she had served as guide and interpreter to the great explorer, and had helped him persuade Montezuma to yield to him, she became known as *"la Providence de la armée de Cortés."*

It was her antecedent story, however, the Cinderella-like degradation which prepared for her later miraculous success, that made her legendary—and perhaps convinced

Shakespeare that no better name could be given to the heroine of *Pericles,* who like the first Marina triumphs over adversity against the greatest of odds. Malintzin-Marina had been sold into slavery by her own mother after that unnatural woman had made a second marriage; she was given by her first master to the Spanish adventurer, who picked her out from among nineteen other slave girls included in the same gift; and she lived long enough to see her son become a captain in the imperial armies that had conquered her people.

For the Latin-American, unlike his northern brethren of the United States and Canada, the Indian problem demands no sacramental or superhuman solution, only a standard sort of acceptance and accommodation—for which reason, his Pocahontas is neither a wife nor a saint (not even, like the romantic's Sacajawea, a pure and silent lover), merely a somewhat exotic mistress, able to function as a go-between in matters of diplomacy and war.

The Roman Catholic Catherine and the Latin American Marina have, however, seemed even less satisfactory than Pocahontas or Sacajawea as archetypal substitutes for the white wife of the refugee American Male. It is not marriage to or congress with, much less worship of the Indian Maiden that he seeks when he flees, or dreams of fleeing, from the settlement and Dame Van Winkle into the wilderness, a world without women at all. And it is partly for this reason that the most authentic American spokesmen have cried "lie" to the Pocahontas legend: "lie" meaning in this case someone else's fantasy, Richardsonian as opposed to Rousseau-istic sentimentality. What is most remarkable about the Pocahontas myth, finally, is not the ease with which it is turned into stereotype—which is true also, as we have noticed, of the legend of Rip Van Winkle—but the frequency and fury with which it has been exposed.

There is, to be sure, a tendency everywhere in the Western world to create a literature of Masculine Protest (often given such honorific names as "realism" or "verism" or "naturalism") by debunking and parodying either women's own literature of self-pity and self-glorification or earlier male idealizations of the opposite sex. Reflecting on this development in classical French realism, the tradition which began with Flaubert and Maupassant and Zola, James Joyce once speculated: "Modern realism is perhaps a reaction. The great French Nation, which venerates the legend of the Maid of Orleans, nevertheless disfigures her through the mouth of Voltaire, lasciviously defiles her in the hands of the engravers of the nineteenth century, riddles and shreds her in the twentieth century. . . ." But acute as this observation is, it is set in too narrow a context, since whatever image of adored womanhood any culture proposes is fair game for the male debunkers: the *Princesse lointaine* or the *donna angelicata*, the Blessed Virgin herself or Richardson's Pamela—in the case of American literature, Pocahontas, who is our Pucelle.

From John Brougham's first effective parody of her legend in 1855 to the series of anti-Pocahontases beginning in 1960 with John Barth's *The Sot-Weed Factor* (which constitute, as we shall see, the very heart of the New Western), such travesties have appeared in an unbroken line of descent; even Herman Melville mocked her by implication, putting in the mouth of one of the most hypocritical scoundrels in *The Confidence Man* the fulsome phrases: "Indians I have always heard to be one of the finest of primitive races, possessed of many heroic virtues. Some noble women, too. When I think of Pocahontas, I am ready to love Indians." But the two most notable attacks on the Pocahontas myth in the nineteenth century came from Henry Adams and Mark Twain—one the full-fledged onslaught of a historian, the other the ironical aside of a novelist. Henry Adams' effort appeared in the guise of a review of a new edition of John Smith's *A True Relation of Virginia* in the *Atlantic Monthly* for January, 1867, and was later reprinted in *Chapters of Erie*. "The question raised," Adams insists, "is upon the veracity of Captain John Smith"; and he concludes that the whole belatedly hoked-up account of the Captain's rescue by Pocahontas, though a "most romantic episode," is creditable neither to Smith's "veracity or his honor."

Obviously, it is first of all as a scholar, a student of "facts" to whom Smith's belated addition to his memoirs is clearly spurious, that Adams finds the Pocahontas story "mendacious." But surely there is a sense, too, in which he must think it "untrue" as Plato considered Homer's accounts of the gods of Greece "untrue": i.e., false to the deepest meanings of life as he understood them, and doing no one any good to believe.

To this view Mark Twain seems to subscribe, too, though the ironies he brings to bear on the fantastic revision of the legend contained in *Pudd'nhead Wilson* are complex to the point of confusion—like so much else in that mad and wonderful book. The voice in which he retells the tale is that of Roxana, an octaroon slave-woman, trying by the recital of his mythological pedigree to shame into action her no-good son, whom she has passed off as white, but who has just evaded a duel.

"Whatever has come o' yo' Essex blood? Dat's what I can't understan'," she says, referring to Cecil Burleigh Essex, the F.F.V. gentlemen whose very name is a roll call of Elizabethan dignitaries, and who has fathered on her the illegitimate boy she is addressing. "En it ain't on'y jist Essex blood dat's in you, not by a long sight—'deed it ain't! My great-great-great-gran'father en yo' great-great-great-great-gran'father was ole Cap'n John Smith, de highest blood dat Ole Virginny ever turned out, en *his* great-great-gran'mother or somers along back dah, was Pocahontas de Injun queen, en her husbun' was a nigger king outen Africa—en yit here you is, a slinkin' outen a duel en disgracin' our whole line like an ornery low-down hound!" But it is the Negroes, we notice, who represent the Smith-Pocahontases in this line of descent, in which the good Captain himself becomes the offspring of both those colored races in whose presence White Americans have lived out their destiny; while the aristocratic pretensions and the fear of miscegenation of Virginia gentlemen are simultaneously mocked.

Yet in a strange way, Twain's Roxana represents a fulfillment as well as a mockery of the myth spawned by John Smith's self-congratulatory lies; for she is herself a kind of reborn Pocahontas, whatever her color (in fact, she looks White, and is a Negro by mythological definition of the community just as she is an Indian by her own). This time, however, she is Mistress and Mother rather than Maiden—a fully sexual Pocahontas, thanks to her one-eighth Negro blood; and, as the mother of the mother of the mother of Smith, archetypally speaking, the Great Mother of us all. In the very last pages of the book, to be sure, she capitulates to the White Man's God, crying out, "De Lord have mercy on me, po' misable sinner dat I is!" But up to that point, slave though she may be, she has seemed herself just such a fertility goddess as those at whose shrine men once prayed for potency and love. And in this sense, Twain has anticipated certain uses of Pocahontas that did not really flourish until the twentieth century.

THE BASIC MYTHS, III:
TWO MOTHERS OF US ALL

POCAHONTAS HAS BEEN caricatured and exposed by many serious American writers in pursuit of what they fondly consider "reality" as opposed to myth. She has also been—though perhaps never quite successfully—transformed into a Pop Art heroine, the sort of campy Earth Goddess or Great Mother familiar to us these days in those Anna Magnani types projected by Tennessee Williams, or more recently in Andy Warhol's version of Marilyn Monroe. The history of this particular attempt at kidnapping an idol from the White Protestant Mamas and reinventing her as the dream-girl of their often homosexual, and invariably antifeminist, sons has a long shadowy history, which provides a paradigm of the whole process of cultural inversion, sometimes called Camp.

In the case of Pocahontas, not only Twain but, more unexpectedly, Walt Whitman anticipates the process, which, after the intervention of Carl Sandburg and Vachel Lindsay, reaches a climax in Hart Crane's *The Bridge*. Its coming to full awareness, however, depends on the first wave of White self-hatred and adulation of colored men which swept England and the United States in the twenties. Like the second wave, now upon us, it was accompanied by a certain brand of anti-Semitism and a studied hostility to traditional notions of maturity. Wyndham Lewis in *Pale-Face* (the only full-scale study of the First Wave) associates it with Communist politics, as well as with what he calls "the child cult" and the "homo-motive"; but his book, shrill, almost hysterical, and everywhere marred by Fascist apologetics, is out of print and unread. Nonetheless, we cannot understand the post-World War I cult of Pocahontas without some sense of the period—and especially of its relationship to Walt Whitman, whom Lewis calls, wickedly but not unaptly, "the Father of the American Baby."

Whitman does not mention Pocahontas by name, since, on principle, he avoids evoking all the named figures out of popular American mythology, except for Columbus. Yet the image of an anti-genteel Indian Maiden, salvational *because* sexual, begins first to emerge in his lines: "I saw the marriage of the trapper in the open air in the far west, the bride was a red girl . . . She had long eyelashes, her head was bare, her coarse straight locks descended upon her voluptuous limbs and reach'd to her feet."

Among the early twentieth century Whitmanians, the image of this voluptuous Indian girl recurs and is identified with the favorite Indian of their mothers and aunts, Pocahontas. Carl Sandburg strikes the keynote once and for all, though in passing: "Pocahontas' body, lovely as a poplar, sweet as a red haw in November, or a paw-paw in May. . . ." And the *naked* Pocahontas, so long-denied though hinted at in Smith himself and fixed in a whirling image by William Strachey, strives to be reborn, the "wanton young girle" whose name meant "frisky," and behind her the Indian Queen of the sixteenth century engravers, with her evocation of an even remoter woodland Ceres or Aphrodite. Stripped of the stiff Jacobean garb in which Rolfe insisted that she be painted, how oddly Pocahontas is—not only in her nudity, but in her association with the magic crop of tobacco—like that naked Daughter of Manito of which a score of Indian tales tell.

According to one version, the lost hunters lucky enough to come upon her in a secluded valley were directed by signs to return a year later to the place where she had been sitting—a hand on either side to sustain the weight of her reclining, naked body. And returning, they discovered corn sprouting where her right palm had rested, beans where her left hand had pressed the ground, and tobacco where her divine ass had touched the earth.

It is just such a woodland Ceres whom Vachel Lindsay invokes in a poem called "Our Mother Pocahontas," itself directly inspired by the lines from Sandburg. And celebrating her, Lindsay finds an occasion for denying not only his own White mother, but his White father as well:

> The Forest, arching low and wide
> Gloried in its Indian bride . . .
> John Rolfe is not our ancestor.
> We rise from out the soul of her. . . .

It is a valedictory poem he is writing, a farewell by an American to the Europe which has produced him.

> We here renounce our Saxon blood . . .
> We here renounce our Teuton pride;
> Our Norse and Slavic boasts have died:
> Italian dreams are swept away,
> And Celtic feuds are lost today. . . .

What a lovely American dream—to be reborn as a fatherless Indian boy from a husbandless Indian mother, to have no father at all, except for the Forest itself: all fear of miscegenation washed away in the same cleansing metaphor that washes away our European ancestry.

In 1967, at any rate, an analogous dream of disavowing one's whiteness and becoming all Indian still possesses the minds of poets—Gary Snyder, for instance, writing:

> A CURSE
> ON THE MEN IN WASHINGTON, PENTAGON
>
> OM A KA TA TA PA YA SA SVAHA
>
> As you shoot down the Vietnamese girls and men
>   in their fields
>   Burning and chopping,
>   Poisoning and blighting.

So surely I hunt the white man down
    in my heart.
The crew-cutted Seattle boy
The Portland boy who worked for U.P.
        that was me.

I won't let him live. The "American"
    I'll destroy. The "Christian"
        has long been dead.

They won't pass on to my children.
I'll give them Chief Joseph, the bison herds,
Ishi, sparrowhawk, the fir trees,
The Buddha, their own naked bodies,
Swimming and dancing and singing
        instead.

As I kill the white man
    the "American"
        in me
And bring out the ghost dance:
To bring back America, the grass and the streams,

To trample your throat in your dreams.

This magic I work, this loving I give
    That my children may flourish

And yours won't live.

HI' NISWA' VITA' KI' NI

And this is where Crane began when he made his big try—his attempt to create a super-Whitmanian poem complete with all the mythological names Walt himself had rejected. It is this Pocahontas—the Indian maid out of Sandburg by Vachel Lindsay—whom Crane's Rip Van

Winkle dreams in his flight from civilization to the wilderness of his own head:

> Pocahontas, bride—
> O Princess whose brown lap was virgin May . . .
> I left the village for dogwood, By the canoe
> Tugging below the mill-race, I could see
> Your hair's keen crescent running. . . .

The section of the poem in which these lines appear is called "The Dance," and not only constitutes the true center of *The Bridge*, but is also the passage which has most influenced other art: turned to music by Aaron Copland in a piece entitled "Appalachian Spring," and later notably choreographed by Martha Graham, in whom the New Pocahontas became at last living flesh.

"Here," Crane himself explains, commenting on the passage to Otto Kahn, "one is on the pure mythical and smoky soil at last! Not only do I describe the conflict between the two races in this dance—I also become identified with the Indian and his world, before it is over."

"*His* world," Crane says, and the "his" is a giveaway, a revelation that the poet has not been telling quite his own truth in his adaptation of the myth of Pocahontas—that what he yearns to celebrate is not the legendary Indian Princess at all, much less John Smith, but the dusky Indian Prince whom he imagines his as well as her true lover. Indeed, Crane's name for that dusky Prince comes out of his own private mythological store, "Maquokeeta" having been the actual middle name of a cabdriver boy friend; and it is to him, not to Pocahontas, that the poet chants the phallic song in which his verse—elsewhere flaccid and unconvincing—comes to life:

> Dance, Maquokeeta! snake that lives before,
> That casts his pelt, and lives beyond! Sprout, horn!
> Spark, tooth! Medicine-man, relent, restore—
> Lie to us—dance us back the tribal morn!

It seems an apt enough phrase for summing up our long relationship to the American myth most often and most passionately branded a hoax. "Lie to us." Lie.

To call the lie a lie, however, is to speak the truth; and the truth proved for Crane a charm, releasing him from sentimentality to passion. Even as his retelling of the myth became phallic rather than idyllic, it was converted from the story of a reassuring rescue to the account of a terrifying assault. The stone axe poised harmless in the hand of the Redskin killer falls at last after three hundred years, though this time on an Indian head; or rather it is transformed into a flight of deadly arrows, as Maquokeeta ceases to be a Prince and becomes an unredeemable victim, St. Sebastian (patron saint of the homosexuals) and Hart Crane in one:

> And buzzard-circulated, screamed from the stake;
> I could not pick the arrows from my side.
> Wrapped in that fire, I saw more escorts wake—
> Flickering, spring up the hill, groins like a tide.

But Crane cannot hold it here, submitting as the poem moves on to one more disconcerting metamorphosis, which turns Pocahontas into a White mama down on the farm in Indiana. The name of the state is the name of the next section, whose introductory marginal gloss says: ". . . and read her in a mother's farewell gaze," and whose final absurd stanza speaks in that mother's voice:

> Come back to Indiana—not too late!
>   (Or will you be a stranger to the end?)
> Good-bye . . . Good-bye . . . Oh, I shall always wait
>   You, Larry, traveler—
>   stranger,
>   son,
>   —my friend—

But the notion of the WASP mother as friend to her son is utterly alien to our dearest dreams; and the identification of her with Pocahontas betrays the disavowal of the European past for which the Indian Princess essentially stands. How can Dame Van Winkle and Powhatan's daughter be blended into one? Our White mothers themselves would have scorned such an idea, since they have always dreamed themselves and Indians irreconcilable enemies, as the myth of Hannah Duston sufficiently testifies. Indeed, it might be best to think of that legend as portraying a second or rival Great Mother of Us All, incapable of occupying the same archetypal world as the first.

But most often, Hannah's story is thought of as being just one more account of Indian captivity; and Cotton Mather, first eminent American author to retell it (he was followed by Nathaniel Hawthorne and Henry David Thoreau), includes it in that category in his *Magnalia Christi Americana*. But, in fact, three out of four of our basic myths deal with that theme—all, that is to say, except Rip Van Winkle—and to emphasize this point of resemblance rather than their more important differences would be misleading.

What does matter is that the myths invented by John Smith and the trapper Alexander Henry, though both begin with a capture, end by celebrating the love which mitigates rather than the hate which fosters the state of war between White and Red out of which they arise. The male imagination, for better or for worse, tends to transform the tale of captivity into one of adoption, to substitute the male dream of joining the Indians for the female fantasy of being dragged off by them. Rip Van Winkle's daughter Judith, we remember, when confronted by the disappearance of her father, could imagine nothing else than that he was "carried away by the Indians"; while Huck Finn is telling us the minute his trials with Jim are over: "And then Tom he talked along, and talked along, and says, let's all three slide out of here, one of these nights, and get an outfit, and go for howling adventures amongst the Injuns, over in the Territory, for a couple of weeks or so; and I says, all right, that suits me. . . ."

With the Tom-Huck fantasy every reader of our classic books is familiar and sympathetic, but the opposing Dream of Women he is likely to find baffling as well as unappealing; and, indeed, the story of Hannah Duston seems to have faded from the popular mind since this century began. It was not always so, however, for as late as June 17, 1874, a statue was being unveiled, with appropriate ceremonies, in Haverhill, Massachusetts: the stone figure of a long-skirted, sunbonneted woman with a tomahawk raised aloft in her delicate hand—so like the standard Freudian dream of a castrating mother that it is hard to believe it has not been torn down long since by some maimed New England male just out of analysis.

The poet laureate of the unveiling was disturbed by no Freudian second thoughts, at any rate, singing blithely in verses which have been somehow preserved:

> To a gift from the sculptor's graphic hand,—
> An emblem glorious and grand,
> Unveiled to the world for aye to stand,—
>   Old Mother Duston. . . .

and assuring his audience that not "Old Mother Duston" alone, but many like her, an endless line of mothers, have stood just so staunchly over us with upraised axe and unfaltering gaze:

> We've come inspired of the fond old mothers.
> Their sainted care still o'er us hovers,
> Daring in deeds transcending others
>   Mid life's relations. . . .

Reading these lines, we understand that, on a first level of consciousness at least, the uplifted tomahawk in mother's hand is not intended to maim us poor sons at all, but only to protect us against the evil marauder, the bogey-man, the Bad Father, identified in our world with the Indian. Or perhaps we are supposed to assume that the weapon eternally at the ready is intended to avenge us, for the skull of the American boy-baby has already been cracked against a tree trunk before Mother is driven to violence—has, indeed been thus smashed from the beginning of American time. There is no doubt, at any rate, that one of the most compelling recurrent images in the legends of Indian warfare (indeed, in our whole legendary heritage) is that of the just-born babe, a son snatched from his mother's milky breast, and swung by the heels—in a Red fist, of course—against a nearby tree trunk, even as that mother is being dragged off into slavery.

How that bloody picture has possessed the female imagination for more than three centuries, and how it appears over and over everywhere in our literature: from Cotton Mather himself ("In fine when the *children* of the *English Captives* cried at any time . . . the manner of the *Indian* was to dash out their brains against a *Tree*"); to Anna Eliza Bleeker's novel—published only four years after the framing of the American Constitution—*The History of Maria Kittle,* in which the Indians are portrayed as snatching Maria's "laughing babe" and dashing "his little forehead," this time "against the stones"; to Robert Penn Warren's *Brother to Dragons,* a long narrative poem published in 1953, in which the author puts into the mouth of Thomas Jefferson, merely as a simile by the way, the following lines:

> Listen, the Indian, when some poor frontier mother,
>   a captive, lags
> By the trail to feed her brat, he'll snatch its heels
> And snap the head against a tree trunk, like a whip.
> Just so, and the head pops like an egg. . . .

Side by side, however, with this image of a primal offense against motherhood and the helpless son is another, as omnipresent if not as central to the meaning of the myth of Indian Captivity as the first. In the second, the White woman appears alone, no longer a mother but an object of lust, usually portrayed as running the gauntlet naked, or tied naked to the stake and surrounded by howling Redskins; and this time, female nakedness, because it is White rather than Red, is intended to symbolize horror rather than redeeming passion. In the sort of dime novel dealing with the plight of WASP females among the Indians but aimed at WASP male readers, these images are turned into crude illustrations.

As early as 1794 (only a year after *Maria Kittle* had titillated the female audience), there appeared in an edition of *The Affecting History . . of Frederic Manheim's Family* an engraving which purported to show Frederic's daughters stripped to the buff and lashed to the stake, while a horde of Indians danced wildly about them. And, indeed, this primordial image has continued to haunt pulp fiction ever since (often adorning the covers of magazines devoted to it); for it panders to that basic White male desire at once to relish and deplore, vicariously share and publicly condemn, the rape of White female innocence. To be sure, as the generations have gone by, the color of her violators has changed, though that of the violated woman has remained the same: from the Red of the Indians with whom it all began, to the Yellow of such malign Chinese as Dr. Fu Manchu, the Black of those Africans who stalk so lubriciously through the pages of Edgar Rice Burroughs' Tarzan books, or the Purple or Green Martians who represent the crudest fantasy level of science fiction.

Whatever the acutal habits of Chinese, Africans, and Martians in this regard, the American Indians, as we have already observed, did not comply. Yet the myth demanded it; and so, many of the early accounts of female captivity without actually lying hint darkly about the sexual fate of their victims—depending on the imagination of their readers to fill in the discreet blanks more luridly than did life itself.

Occasionally, however, the author of such a narrative is moved to speak frankly, even at the risk of losing audience interest. In the early eighteenth century captivity story called *God's Mercy Surmounting Man's Cruelty, as Exemplified in the Captivity and Surprising Deliverance of Elizabeth Hanson,* etc., etc., for instance, we read: "The Indians are very civil towards their captive women, not offering any incivility by any indecent carriage (unless they be much overcome in liquor), which is commendable in them so far." But even so serious and ambitious a writer as Joel Barlow preferred to play up what sub-sexual atrocities the Indians were willing to provide along these lines—the standard stripping of female captives (apparently prompted by a desire for their garments rather than their flesh), and especially the baring of their breasts, then as now an item which sold books. A few lines from Barlow's poem on the abduction and murder by Indians of a certain Miss Jane McCrea, whom he rechristens Lucinda for poetic purposes, will give a fair notion of the prevailing techniques:

> Two Mohawks met the maid—historian hold!—
> She starts with eyes upturned and fleeting breath,
> In their raised axes views her instant death.
> Her hair, half lost along the shrubs she passed,
> Rolls, in loose tangles, round her lovely waist;
> Her kerchief torn betrays the globes of snow
> That heave responsive to her weight of woe.
> With calculating pause and demon grin
> They seize her hands, and through her face divine
> Drive the descending axe. . . .

Such images, which begin with suggestions of rape and end in the fact of murder, are, however, essentially male fantasies—part of the male attempt to kidnap archetypal material originally intended for female consumption. Women will, to be sure, endure a *touch* of prurience, the merest hint of threatened violation in the total tale of their indignities, just as they will submit to a certain amount of piety on the part of male divines, retelling their adventures from the pulpit like Cotton Mather, to glorify a paternalistic God. They will even accept a modicum of philosophizing about the evil nature of the Indians—allow their mythologized histories to be used as evidence against the presumed teachings of Rousseau. So they were used, at any rate, by one Archibald Loudon, who wrote in a preface to a collection of such narratives published in 1808: "The philosopher who speaks with delight, of the original simplicity, and primitive innocence of mankind, may here learn, that man, uncivilized and barbarous, is worse than the most ferocious wolf. . . ."

But women insist that their *essential fable* be not obscured by such irrelevant male concerns, that the story remain true to their central vision of their lot and be projected in terms of their own sort of heroine: a strong but immensely ordinary woman—preferably a mother—who is confronted by a male antagonist and, finding no male champion, must deliver herself. The very names of the captives, memorialized in scores of collections and anthologies, are, in their homeliness, their lack of glamor, representative enough to seem invented: Mery Jemison and Mary Rowlandson and Mary Johnson and Mary Kinnan, and Elizabeth Hanson and Mercy Harbison and Hannah Swarton and Hannah Duston.

What is most important is not (though it recommends itself for consideration to any lover of symbols) the repeated appearance of the name of the Mother of God, which Anna Eliza Bleeker appears to have responded to in calling the heroine of her fictional captivity narrative Maria Kittle. What really counts is the composite image created finally in any mind which tries to evoke one by one the succession of Marys and Mercys and Elizabeths and Hannahs—all, we are somehow sure, utterly un-exotic, completely non-alluring, objects of lust only to the eyes of those no better than beasts. Together they constitute the true anti-Pocahontas: our other—alas, realer—mother, the Great WASP Mother of Us All, who, far from achieving a reconciliation between White men and Red, turns the weapon of the Indian against him in a final act of bloodshed and vengeance.

It does not matter to the mythmakers that not all of the women captured by the Indians in the days of border warfare actually found their captors disagreeable, that some of them, in fact, preferred to remain with those who had snatched them away by force. Such a figure as Mery Jemison remains mythologically inert precisely because she married Red, wed not one but two Indians, and produced several children who became leaders in their tribe. History may record, but legend does not choose to remember, that she finally went native enough nearly to forget her own English tongue, and to look on coolly as the entrails of a White captive were drawn out through a small hole in his belly by the people into whom she had married. She remains as irrelevant as those eccentric males who resented rather than rejoiced in their captivity; or the celebrated line of Indian haters which stretches all the way from the Colonel Moredock recalled in Melville's *The Confidence Man* to Tom Quick, whose adventures in pulp editions fired the fancies of generations of bloodthirsty boys, but compelled the imagination of no major American writer.

Just as the deep male memory returns compulsively to stories of men hailed as sons by dusky chieftains or as brothers by swarthy warriors, smeared with the blood of their fellows, so the female memory lingers *not* on the long life of Miss Jemison, the White Woman of the Genesee, but on such bloody exploits as those performed on April 20, 1788, by the wife of a certain ill-fated James Merrill. That unfortunate husband of a heroine, the record tells us, hearing noises outside his cabin,

> stepped to the door to see what he could discover, and received three musket-balls, which caused him to fall back into the house with a broken leg and arm. The Indians rushed on to the door, but it being instantly fastened by his wife, who, with a girl of about fifteen years of age, stood against it, the Savages could not immediately enter. They broke one part of the door, and one of them crowded partly through. The heroic mother, in the midst of her screaming children and groaning husband, seized an axe, and gave a fatal blow to the savage, and he falling headlong into the house, the others supposing they had gained their end, rushed

after him, until four of them fell in like manner before they discovered their mistake.

The whole Duston myth is embryonically present in that anecdote: male and female, each cast in the appropriate archetypal role (the "heroic mother" and the "groaning husband"), even the archetypal weapon—that "axe" which belongs properly to the Indian's world rather than the White Man's. And that myth, it becomes clear immediately, is an oddly American, which is to say, peculiarly feminist, recasting of the Old World archetype of the Persecuted Maiden: the Damsel in Distress, the Lady carried off by an Ogre or Monster or Dragon.

What makes the story American is not merely that the Ogre has become an Indian, or a "Savage" as the old chronicles prefer to say, but that the Maiden has to deliver herself. Any nearby male is either ineffectual—like poor Merrill, knocked out before the action really begins—or inappropriately reasonable.

"Why don't you put down that axe, dear?" other "groaning" husbands seem to have recommended to their heroic wives—if the old stories can be believed; "it'll just cause more trouble in the end." And sometimes, of course, "those men" are simply not there. It is the familiar soap opera pattern, followed still on television or in the Mary Worth comic strips, in which all males fall into one of two categories: if strong and potent, they are vicious—which means, in mythical terms, Indians; if virtuous, they are hopelessly weak—which means, in mythical terms, husbands.

The vision of males as either threats or encumbrances, but never heroic deliverers is, of course, the invention of females; but American males tend to concur—at least the kind of males who make our classic books and perpetuate our enduring myths. They suggest, however, that the representatives of their sex are absent from such encounters as Mrs. Merrill's brush with the Redskins because they are off fighting quite other monsters—who have in their power no female prisoners at all. Sometimes those other monsters are disconcertingly White, like Herman Melville's Moby Dick, for instance; and we are inclined to suspect that they may have absorbed the White Mother into their bulky and threatening selves. Sometimes, on the other hand, the enemies of the male are satisfactorily dark in hue, like the natives in Edgar Allan Poe's *Gordon Pym,* for instance; but even in such cases, it turns out that they simply have not happened to take any White females captive.

There is a kind of stereotypical middle ground between male and female—occupied by books like Fenimore Cooper's *Leatherstocking Tales*—in which Damsels in Distress are quite properly rescued by junior officers in uniform. But in our truly archetypal literature there are only females delivering themselves from monsters, and/or males killing monsters who guard no females. Or still worse—and this tends to be the case in our very greatest books—those males may be portrayed as lolling about, at least in their dreams, with the very Savages whom their mothers, daughters, and wives, in corresponding nightmares at least, are trying to escape or even planning to slay.

It is well to remember in this context that the famous tomahawk, taken up by desperate women against those who customarily wield it, also doubles as a tobacco pipe, the famous pipe of peace, shared by many a White man and his dark-skinned brother, even as Ishmael and Queequeg share it in *Moby Dick:* "Soon I proposed a social smoke; and, producing his pouch and tomahawk, he quietly offered me a puff. And then we sat exchanging puffs from that wild pipe of his, and keeping it regularly passing between us."

We are long away from that other use of the tomahawk, for which Mrs. Duston proved to have such an affinity: ". . . she arose before daybreak, and awoke her nurse and the boy, and taking the Indians' tomahawks, they killed them all in their sleep. . . ." It is the climactic episode in a terrifying story, whose major events are not hard to reconstruct, despite the mythologizing which began almost immediately. On March 15, 1697, a small band of Indians descended on the English settlement at Haverhill, Massachusetts, killing some of the settlers and capturing others. They were good Roman Catholics, these Indians (it was, after all, seventeen years after the holy death of Catherine Tekakwitha), who did not forget daily family prayers even in the midst of the wilderness; and, in a sense, their foray was an incident in the war between France and England, or even in that larger religious conflict between Northern and Southern Europe which had been going on ever since the Reformation.

But this is not the way in which our mythological imagination has preserved it, or that Thomas Duston experienced it, seeing the savages who haunted his dreams emerge from the woods into a clearing where he was at work. An indecisive man, and apparently a fonder father than husband, he plays an odd role at this moment of the legend—ineffectual, peripheral, almost comic—as he runs back and forth trying to decide which of his children to save, finally scooping up seven out of the eight, exchanging a few token shots with the raiding party, and escaping without a scratch to himself, the kids, or, for that matter, the enemy.

Convinced that discretion was the better part of *his* valor, and that his wife, only a week past the birth of their eighth child, was not strong enough to be moved (though later she trekked one hundred and fifty miles through the wilderness in a very few days), Thomas Duston abandoned her, along with the infant and a nurse. That infant was killed almost immediately by having its head dashed against a nearby apple tree (later shown with pride to tourists in the region), while Hannah and her nurse were led off through the forest toward an Indian village where, they were assured, they would be stripped naked, scourged, and made to run the gauntlet.

It was at this point, apparently, that Hannah determined not only to escape, but to kill and scalp her captors—hoping, that is, for a profit as well as safety, since there was a bounty of ten pounds apiece on Redskin scalps. Lacking the technical knowledge necessary for the feat, however, she was forced to make common cause with another prisoner from another settlement, a boy called Samuel Leonardson. Young Leonardson she persuaded to ask one of the male Indians how scalps were in fact taken; and following the advice she received, that very night, she, the boy, and her nurse fell upon their captors and dispatched them all except for a "favorite Indian lad" and a woman whom they succeeded only in wounding badly.

In her excitement Hannah forgot the scalps, but remembering her oversight a little later, she returned, removed them, and carried her bloody trophies ("miraculously" her neighbors said) all the way home.

It is, if not exactly a tragic, at least a sufficiently melodramatic climax—but the tale peters off into comedy and pathos, for once home, Mrs. Duston discovered that the bounty on Indian scalps had been canceled during her absence. And though there were handsome presents from private well-wishers, the fifty pounds she had counted on getting out of public funds were at first denied her. Some time later, however, her husband having proved as ineffective at earning a living as at killing Indians and protecting his wife, they fell on hard times; and he petitioned the provincial government in her name, receiving finally twenty-five pounds for her, along with twelve and a half each for the faithful nurse and the boy who had learned so fast from the Indians. But on this—granting the limitations of poor Thomas Duston—they cannot have lived happily-ever-after for very long.

When Cotton Mather retold this tale for exemplary purposes, he ignored the comic-pathetic ending, eliminated the role of the boy Leonardson completely, toned down the bashing-in of the baby's head against the tree (not even remembering to say that it was an *apple tree*, though this was to seem of special significance to Henry David Thoreau), and told the opening episode involving Mrs. Duston's husband quite perfunctorily. It was the *women* who concerned him chiefly, as the title he gave the story (Article XXV in Book VII of the *Magnalia Christi Americana*) indicates: "A *Notable Exploit, wherein, Dux Faemina Facti.*"

Despite the Latin tag, it was the tradition of Israel which Mather had in mind, and it was to their Biblical prototypes that he tried to assimilate Hannah and her nurse. They were, even in distress, he tells us, like another Hannah before them "in pouring out their souls before the Lord." And at Mrs. Duston's moment of decision, he recalls to us the fierce Hebrew mutilator of her male master and exulter over her enemy, writing, "these women took up a Resolution to intimate [*sic*] the action of Jael upon Sisera. . . ." And when at last the deed is done, his own language shifts into the rhythms and words of the Old Testament, as if what he recounts were a deed of pre-Christian antiquity: "they struck such home Blows upon the Heads of the *Sleeping Oppressors,* that . . . *at the feet* of the poor Prisoners, *they bowed, they fell, they lay down.* . . ."

There was no doubt at all in his mind about the justice of the bloody deed performed by Hannah and her companion; they were for him always "poor women," while their enemies were not only "raging Dragons" but practicing Roman Catholics as well—so that the whole event was clearly a testimony to "the singular Providence of God."

And for those among his readers who remember the Christian injunctions against violence and in favor of forgiveness, Mather provides some Talmudic casuistry: "and being where she had not her own *Life* secured by any *Law* unto her, she thought she was not forbidden by any *Law* to take away the *Life* of the *Murderers* by whom her *Child* had been butchered." All of which prepares us for the really Happy Ending, in which virtue does not have to be its own reward since, Mather informs us, lapsing at this point from high Biblical rhetoric into colloquial ease, "they received many *Presents of Congratulation* from their more private Friends; but none gave 'em a greater Taste of

Bounty than Colonel *Nicholson,* the Governour of *Maryland,* who hearing of their Action, sent 'em a very generous Token of his Favour."

This is the account drawn on by the compilers of the Indian Books of the mid-nineteenth century, those compendia of lore, legend, anthropology, and linguistics which were apparently favorite gift volumes of their time. It is retold, for instance, in 1841 in a book called *Events in Indian History,* by James Wimer, who, after a general word of praise for Mather, describes his account of Hannah Duston as "one of the best written articles of all we have had from his pen."

Wimer's own praise for Hannah is even more extreme than Mather's, since for him she is no longer merely the "poor" instrument of Divine Providence, but a full-fledged "heroine," her actions "heroic conduct," and her life one "always viewed with admiration." There is no religious note in Wimer, who ignores the Roman Catholicism of the Indians; and casuistry is equally absent, since for him Hannah is no longer an Old Testament Prophetess murdering for the sake of the Lord, but a real American interested in glory and profit, a kind of pioneering model of the Great Entrepreneurs to follow: "The heroine, Duston had resolved . . . to return home with such trophies as would clearly establish her reputation for heroism, as well as insure her a bounty from the public."

By way of such secularized retellings of Mather's tale, there has been transmitted to our own time the figure of a triumphant woman considered suitable for children's literature. As late as the 1930's she was celebrated in a chapter called "A Pioneer Woman's Heroism," in an illustrated volume entitled *Real Legends of New England.* This tale, the author assures her young readers, has been "told more often than any other" on a similar theme, but it is an expurgated version she offers them: the image of the child's head smashed against the tree trunk quite gone, the threat of running the gauntlet naked tactfully suppressed, only the absolutely essential violence left. But we learn at last the name of the poor Indian who thought of himself for a few fond days as Hannah's master: Bampico.

How strange to turn back from this utterly adulatory and bowdlerized account of a noble killer in action to another version of Mrs. Duston's feat also prepared for child readers, though one hundred years earlier and by one of America's most eminent novelists, Nathaniel Hawthorne. In May, 1836, Hawthorne published in *The American Magazine for Entertaining and Useful Knowledge,* of which he was one of the editors, an essay called "The Duston Family." The very title is revealing, for Hawthorne, unlike any other teller of the tale, is as interested in Goodman Duston as he is in his wife. Indeed, he spends much time at the beginning and end of his narrative building up the reputation of that overshadowed and unlucky man, portraying him as a loving father with a quiet heroism of his own.

The obverse of this is an ironical undercutting of Hannah, of whom Hawthorne remarks at one point—just after he has described Goodman Duston's strange decision to leave her behind—that "as is not improbable, [her husband] had such knowledge of the good lady's character, as afforded him a comfortable hope that she could hold her own, even in a contest with a whole tribe of Indians." And suddenly we are made aware of what Mather was incapable of knowing (though it was Mather on whom Hawthorne drew, Mather who, despite himself, gave Hawthorne the clue): that Hannah Duston is, after all, just another avatar of the termagant wife, who in a later incarnation becomes Dame Van Winkle. And Hawthorne's tone is ironical in precisely the same way as Irving's.

But before he is through, Hawthorne has abandoned irony of any sort in favor of invective, reminding us of the fact Mather and his followers had all hushed up, that seven of Hannah's victims, scalped in their sleep, were not "sleeping oppressors" at all, but only little children, however Indian. Just as her axe is about to fall, as fall it must to satisfy the logic of the myth, he cries out: "But, Oh, the children! Their skins are red; yet spare them Hannah Duston, spare those seven little ones, for the sake of the seven that have fed at your own breast." And when the fatal tomahawk has fallen, he calls her in impotent anger "this awful woman," "a raging tigress," "a bloody old hag," and wishes her drowned or "sunk head over ears in a swamp" —or, finally, "starved to death in the forest, and nothing ever seen of her again, save her skeleton, with the ten scalps twisted round it for a girdle."

It is a tale that calls on us to choose sides, this almost parabolical account of a woman's vengeance. But there are three sides, after all, not just two: the side of the terrible "heroine Duston," with whom the godly Mather aligned himself; the side of her impotent husband, ancestor of Rip and Dagwood Bumstead, with whom Hawthorne chose to identify ("that tender hearted, yet valiant man," he calls him, and ". . . how different," he observes, "is her renown from his!"); and finally the side of the Indian captor, Mather's "raging Dragon," which is to say, the wild man that lives next to the mild husband at the heart of all American males.

For a full-scale development of the third possibility, we will have to turn to Henry David Thoreau and his odd little book, *A Week on the Concord and Merrimack Rivers,* which first appeared in 1849, though it was apparently written in 1845; it was based on events which had occurred in 1839, when, with his brother, Henry had embarked on a boating excursion that bore them not only along the actual rivers of New England, but also "on the placid current of our dreams floating from past to future."

The work is elegiac in tone, more elegiac presumably than Thoreau had intended at the start, for his brother had died in the years between its inception and completion; and Thoreau himself, barely twenty when he lived its events, had crossed the dividing line of thirty before its publication. *A Week* is more than mere elegy, however, as it is more than a travel book, since in its pages Thoreau attempted to create, some hundred years before Hart Crane, a handbook of American mythology based on "savager, and more primeval aspects of nature than our poets have sung." It seemed clear to him that the European tradition "is only white man's poetry"; and he longed to return to the no-time of myth, before "the white man comes, pale as the dawn, with a load of thought."

It is not thought to which Thoreau aspires, but "the fable," "that universal language" which, he assures us, is able "to satisfy the imagination ere it addresses the understanding." He has no doubt that he can achieve such a language, because he feels himself a poet and knows that the poet is "he who can write some pure mythology today. . . ." And he is certain, too, what the subject matter of the new American mythology has to be: the Indian at the moment of first contact with the White invader. All of his life long, as a matter of fact, he was to pursue the theme of the Indian—never, alas, writing the great book on the subject which he kept promising himself to do, but leaving behind in its stead twelve thick notebooks of accumulated raw data, and crying out the magical name with his last breath: "Indian."

"Indian," was his first word as well as his last, the not-so-secret burden of his earliest published work, in which he evoked not the figure of Pocahontas—as Crane, moved by similar ambitions, was to do after him—but with surer instinct the almost anonymous victims of Hannah Duston. Unlike Hawthorne, he is not interested in her husband at all; indeed, in his version of the story (which is told in the "Thursday" chapter of *A Week*), Goodman Duston gets less space than in any other surviving account, being brushed aside in a single introductory phrase, "She had seen her seven elder children flee with their father. . . ." It was the naked encounter of White Female and Red Male which interested him, and he tried to keep it clean of all irrelevancies.

At the start, however, it is not clear which way his sympathy goes. So subtly does he undercut Hannah, so quietly impugn her lurid feat, that at first we are taken in and think him on Mather's side rather than Hawthorne's.

Hannah and her nurse he picks up at the moment of escape from their captors, two lonely women in a canoe, "lightly clad . . . in the English fashion," he tells us, and, ladies that they are, able to handle their paddles only "unskillfully." But in the bottom of that canoe so ineptly propelled, there are, he reveals next, ". . . the still-bleeding scalps of ten of the aborigines." *First*, we are given the bleeding scalps of the Indians, and only then the account of those earlier indignities which—perhaps, *perhaps*—justified two fashionable and unskillful ladies in taking them.

Step by step, he recapitulates their adventure: the ruse of the English boy, the indiscriminate slaughter, a first escape and the return to get scalps "as proofs of what they had done"; then a second flight through the gloomy and fearsome wilderness, in which only the Indian ("a fabulous wild man to *us*," Thoreau remarks) has left his trace. And at this point, he begins clearly to disengage himself from Hannah and her companions, observing that what was to them "a drear and howling wilderness" was for the Indian "a home, adapted to his nature, and cheerful as the smile of the Great Spirit." But he is, we know, at his mythological core an Indian himself, at home in the unexplored regions where women flinch. And, indeed, as he points out unequivocally only a few pages further on, all poets are Indians and, therefore, enemies to ladies: "The talent of composition is very dangerous—the striking out of the heart of life at a blow, as the Indian takes off a scalp. . . ."

No wonder that the image which comes unbidden to Thoreau's mind when he is describing Hannah's triumphant return, her Happy Ending (complete with the fifty-pound bounty) is one of cosmic disaster, of, indeed, the Fall of Man. "The family of Hannah Duston," he writes, "all assembled alive once more, except the infant whose brains were dashed out against the apple tree, and there have been many who in later times have lived to say that they had eaten of the fruit of that apple tree." It is not just bitter grapes which our American ancestors have eaten to set our teeth on edge, but the fruit of the forbidden tree in the garden of Eden. And lest we had forgotten what kind of tree it was, as Cotton Mather had seemed inexplicably to do, Thoreau reminds us—then clinches the association in his very next sentence, which reads: "This seems a long while ago, and yet it happened since Milton wrote his Paradise Lost."

But what precisely is the "it" that has happened? Is it the Second Fall of Man in the Second Paradise of the New World, which Columbus so firmly believed to be the same as the First? And who is responsible this time around? Thoreau poses these questions directly enough, but answers them very indirectly indeed, moving from the portentous evocation of Paradise Lost to a long digression on the age of the world "according to the Mosaic account."

"It is a wearisome while," he observes, thinking back over those six thousand-odd years, then adds, "And yet the lives of but sixty old women, such as live under the hill . . . are sufficient to reach over the whole ground. Taking hold of hands they would span the interval from Eve to my own mother. A respectable tea party merely—whose gossip would be Universal History."

The associations and what they imply are not hard to follow: "Eve," through whom sin entered the world; "my own mother," through whom I came into the same fallen place; the old women under the hill; Hannah Duston. And it is all made even more explicit when Thoreau identifies certain other notables among the sixty members of his cosmic tea party, beginning with three other mothers—of Columbus, William the Conqueror, Jesus Christ—then certain less maternal and more terrible figures: the dread Cumaean Sybil; Helen who brought Troy down; Queen Semiramis, the most wicked woman who ever lived; and at last, combining the malign and motherly, "the Sixtieth was Eve, the mother of mankind. So much for the *Old woman that lives under the hill, And if she's not gone she lives there still.*" And so much, too, for those Mothers of Us All, whom we have been pursuing from Pocahontas to Hannah Duston.

It is clearly the world of women, which he equates with

the world of history, that is for Thoreau the nightmare world of After the Fall: a dreary world to which we have been expelled from a blithe world for males only, the Dream Garden of America, "cheerful as the smile of the Great Spirit."

Just what that Dream Garden is, however, what Second Paradise was lost when White women entered the American woods that are forever hostile to them to scalp the woodland scalpers with whom the American artist identifies himself—this we cannot learn from the story of Hannah Duston alone. But Thoreau has provided us with the other half of the total myth of the West—the myth of a lost primeval world—telling on Wednesday (a chapter, a day, before the legend of Hannah Duston) his version of a series of adventures that did not occur in history until half a century after the encounter of Hannah and Bampico, and that were not recorded in print until half a century later than that. In terms of the myth, however, the later story is prior to the earlier, as dream is always prior to history; Thoreau, who knew so much, knew this, too.

THE BASIC MYTHS, IV:
IN DREAMS AWAKE

THOREAU BEGINS with a very general reference to Alexander Henry's *Adventures,* the work which provided him a clue to the nature of the American Earthly Paradise, lost when the first White woman entered. "A classic among American books," he calls it, adding by way of explanation that "it reads like the argument to a great poem on the primitive state of the country and its inhabitants, and the reader imagines what in each case, with the invocation of the Muse, might be sung. . . ." But for only one incident out of Henry's entire store does Thoreau invoke his Muse: the encounter between the White fur-trapper, Henry, and the Indian warrior, Wawatam, that grandson of the Serpent, who plays Eve to Henry's Adam in the Eden of the New World.

Actually, the incidents involving Wawatam take up a good many pages of Henry's book, being central to his view of himself and his destiny. He sees himself as one almost miraculously protected in the very midst of the hostilities between White Man and Red. In one place he observes that he had been "preserved so often, and so unexpectedly . . ." that he had been left "with a strong inclination to believe . . . no Indian could do me hurt." It is a view not unlike Captain John Smith's notion of himself, though for Henry, Pocahontas has become a male.

Henry's account covers the sixteen years between 1760 and 1776: in terms of his own life, the period between attaining his majority and passing the midpoint of his allotted three score and ten; in terms of history, the era from the conclusion of the French and Indian Wars to the beginning of the American Revolution. It is a long stretch of time he looks back upon as a man of seventy, rich and retired and safe in Montreal, but he claims to remember vividly every one of his rescuers: an old Indian woman, who hid him in her attic in the midst of drunken rioting at the very start of his adventures; a Pawnee squaw, who did much the same shortly thereafter; a ferocious Brave called Weniway, who unexpectedly offered to adopt him in the place of a dead brother; a war party of Ottawas, who snatched him from an enemy tribe; and, only at last, Wawatam, his male Pocahontas, who saved him not once but three times.

It is Wawatam on whom Thoreau chooses to linger; but Henry seems to find his chief pleasure in remembering himself, that lost young man it obviously delights him to have been, eternally threatened and eternally saved by the dusky warriors who prove always to love him more than they hate his race. No use for him to tell us in his preface that he is merely a cold and objective reporter, that "all comment . . . is studiously avoided." He may not ever judge the Indians, but he judges himself constantly—remarking, for instance, at one point, when in order to pass as an Indian he finds it necessary to cut off his hair: "I parted, not without some regret, with the long hair . . . which I fancied to be ornamental; but the ladies of the family, and of the village in general, appeared to think my person improved, and now condescended to call me handsome. . . ."

As a matter of fact, disguise as well as concealment was a standard part of the strategy by which Henry kept himself so long and so astonishingly safe in hostile territory. Once he disguised himself as a *Canadien*, for instance, and once as a Chippewa. But the latter disguise was fundamentally different from the former—more than a matter of mere convenience—for there is a sense in which Henry, though forced by circumstances to abide among Indians and looking forward always to a prosperous old age in the cities of his own people, *became* at least temporarily an

Indian, confessing in one place: "By degrees, I became familiarized with this kind of life; and had it not been for the idea of which I could not divest my mind, that I was living among savages, and for the whispers of a lingering hope, that I should one day be released from it . . . I could have enjoyed as much happiness in this, as in any other situation."

There is something equivocal here, as there is in most of the archetypal material dealing with the Indian Captivities of males, some indication of an uneasy longing to cast off the burden of being White, and to make of slavery among the Indians a kind of freedom, which is, of course, never to be found in the mythology of female captivity. In the chronicles, we occasionally come upon confessions which go even beyond this—expressions of an almost voluptuous acceptance by certain White captives of their subjugation to an alien race. A chronicler called James Smith, for instance, recalling his own trials among the Indians in the year 1755, reports that a fellow White prisoner he encountered had once cried out to him on behalf of slavery, "It is good for a man to bear the yoke in his youth."

And savoring that odd Biblical phrase, we think perhaps of the sentence out of Crèvecoeur, gleefully evoked by D. H. Lawrence in his *Studies in Classic American Literature* (one more in the eye for Mother!): "There must be something in their [the Indians'] social bond singularly captivating, and far superior to anything to be boasted of among us; for thousands of Europeans are Indians, and we have no examples of even one of the aborigines having from choice become European. . . ."

Lawrence, like Crèvecoeur before him, has forgotten Pocahontas, has he not—all the Pocahontases—concentrating as he does exclusively on males; for the legend sponsored by John Smith becomes precisely an account of the Europeanized Indian, just as the myth adumbrated by Henry becomes an account of the Indianized European.

Henry himself did not *quite* go over to the Indians, never really able to forget that he was a captive among them, and that at any drunken moment (whiskey and drunkenness are everywhere in his account—a sinister *leit-motif*), they might snatch him from the hands of his protectors and make a broth of him to strengthen their own flagging vitality. Only when he shares a pipe with them does Henry seem completely at ease; for even as whiskey divides the races, tobacco joins them. Of this Henry seems well aware, introducing, for example, the scene of parting between himself and Wawatam by telling the reader: ". . . my father and brother (for he was alternately each of these) lit his pipe and presented it to me, saying 'My son, this may be the last time that ever you and I shall smoke out of the same pipe!' "

There is a constant contrast, certainly, throughout Henry's book, between the "white man's milk," rum, and the Red Man's medicine, tobacco—between that magical potion that helped Rip escape his wife but could unite him only with the dumb ghosts of the European past and that New World drug (first in the series that has now reached peyote and marijuana) associated with Pocahontas and the Daughter of Manito behind her, the gift of the Good Companion whom the runaway son-husband finds in the woods, the pledge of their troth.

When Thoreau, who never smoked anything stronger than dried lily-bulbs and that only as a boy, retells the tale of Alexander Henry and Wawatam, he leaves out tobacco completely, understanding neither its power to intoxicate nor its role in the ritual of male communion. And his only reference to whiskey is so ambiguous that it must be misunderstood by all but close readers of the original chronicle, or long-time students of Indian customs. "If Wawatam would taste the 'white man's milk' with his tribe," Thoreau writes, "or take his bowl of human broth made of the trader's fellow countrymen, he first finds a place of safety for his Friend. . . ." And it sounds as if "milk" and "broth" are synonyms for each other, both belonging to that exotic vice of cannibalism with which, from the very start, those first Wild Indians, the Caribs, had been associated. That cannibalism Thoreau does not play down at all; but what does disappear from his version of the story—along with the tobacco and rum—is any suggestion that Henry is a captive, that his association with Wawatam is anything but voluntary on both sides, *given*—as it were—from the first.

Henry, on the other hand, builds the relationship gradually, describing three separate appearances of Wawatam: one to declare his comradeship in time of peace, one to warn Henry of impending disaster, one to rescue him and take him into protective custody in time of war. "He commenced a speech," Henry says of the first occasion, "in which he informed me that some years before, he had observed a fast, devoting himself . . . to solitude, and to the mortification of his body, and . . . that on this occasion, he had dreamed of adopting an Englishman, as his son, brother and friend; that from the moment in which he first beheld me, he had recognized me as the person whom the Great Spirit had been pleased to point out to him for a brother. . . ." The second time, we learn, Wawatam says cryptically that "he himself had been frequently disturbed with *the noise of evil birds*"; but the warning seems to have been too oblique, for it goes unheeded. And the third time, we are permitted to hear Wawatam make a long speech on behalf of his captured and helpless friend, a moving oration which ends: "He is my brother; and because I am your relation, he is therefore your relation, too:—and how, being your relation, can he be your slave?"

All of this Thoreau collapses in time, compresses into a single incident, to suit the context of the long essay on Friendship which is the heart of his Wednesday chapter and to emphasize its dreamlike, mythical quality. Henry himself, whose book is shot through with dreams and dream interpretation, remarks once that his own adventures struck him as "more like dreams than realities, more like fiction than truth." But to Thoreau, Henry's style seems to betray the fantastic nature of its subject, being finally the style of one who "writes for the information of his readers, for science, and for history."

What he himself is after, he informs us, is "not the *annals* of the country, but the . . . perennials, which are without date. When out of history the truth shall be extracted, it will have shed its dates like withered leaves." Such an extraction of higher truth out of lower history he attempts to perform by turning the ordeal of Henry into an Idyll, not just in its happier moments, but throughout.

The center of the Idyll, he recognizes, is the relationship of Henry and Wawatam, stripped down to its essentials: an archetypal story central to the American experience, an inexhaustible source of what Thoreau himself calls "satisfaction and security," the memory of a Paradise never really quite lost, even after evil Woman had come between the White woodsman and the Red offspring of the Serpent whom he had found "a help meet for him."

> The stern, imperturbable warrior, after fasting, solitude and mortification of body, comes to the white man's lodge, and affirms that he is the white brother whom he saw in his dream, and adopts him henceforth. He buries the hatchet as it regards his friend, and they hunt and feast and make maple sugar together.

Among Indians, men do not in fact make maple sugar, as Henry's own account takes pains to point out; but Thoreau is in need of another mythological tree to set against Hannah Duston's bitter apple tree. And that tree he finds in the sugar maple, native to the American forest, an uncultivated source of sweetness and nourishment—which, in his private mythology, provides an absolute contrast to the imported apple tree, sign of the family homestead, as well as symbol twice over (once as Genesis reminds us, once as Newton noticed in his orchard) of the Fall.

But the "undisturbed and happy intercourse" of the White and Red male friends (it is thus finally that Thoreau denominates Henry's ambiguous captivity) cannot last. Reasons which Thoreau never makes clear, since making them clear would demand revealing that their association is not altogether voluntary, compel the two to part; and we are granted a last sight of Wawatam praying to the Kitchi Manito for his brother in a passage quoted directly from Alexander Henry's *History*. "Brother" is the description of their relationship which Thoreau prefers, expurgating the reference to them as adoptive father and son, since it does not fit his mythological view. And it is well, finally, that Thoreau offers us no convincing historical explanation for Henry's expulsion from his Earthly Paradise, since this permits him to suggest an archetypal one, or at least persuade us to supply it by drawing on our memories of what happened between Hannah and Bampico in her wilderness, which is mythologically only another part of the same forest.

"Friendship is not so kind as it is imagined," Thoreau continues after he has dismissed Wawatam with the valedictory phrase, "We never hear of him again"; and at first we are not sure what he is after. "Friendship is not so kind as it is imagined . . . it has not much human blood in it, but consists with a certain disregard for men and their erections . . ." It is passionless, he is trying to tell us surely, this "happy intercourse" and, therefore, something more or less than human. But the word "erections" is a pun, signifying "monuments" as well as risings of the flesh, and the sentence swings another way on its pivot: ". . . a certain disregard for men and their erections, the Christian duties and humanities."

"We may call it an essentially heathenish intercourse . . . ," Thoreau continues, which prompts him to add: "When the Friend comes out of his heathenism . . . when he forgets his mythology and treats his Friend like a Christian . . . then Friendship . . . becomes charity; that principle which established the almshouse is now beginning with its charity at home, and establishing an almshouse and pauper relations there."

Here, then, is the real point at last. It is a *Pagan* Paradise Regained that Americans have dreamed in the forests of the New World, a natural Eden lost when Christianity intervened—which means when woman intervened, when Hannah Duston appeared, with her righteousness and sexual fears, the gloomy figure of Cotton Mather following close behind her, ready to justify her killer-role with appropriate scriptural quotations.

There are, finally, two archetypal versions of the Fall in the Garden: one inherited from the Old World, one created in the New. In the first, Man and Woman are portrayed living at peace in an Earthly Paradise until the Serpent enters; in the second, Man and the Serpent are presented as cohabiting amicably until Woman comes on the scene. For the Indian *is* the serpent—not only to the orthodox Christian imagination, to which the savages are "fierce Dragons," but to the heterodox mythic mind of Americans as well. We recall that Henry describes Wawatam in one place blowing tobacco smoke toward a presumably offended snake, who, he explains, is his "grandfather."

It is a haunting little episode which recurs in the fiction of William Faulkner twice over, though it is hard to say whether he read it in Alexander Henry, or heard it from some old Indian known in his childhood, or merely dreamed it once more. Each time, however, it is not an Indian who thus greets a snake, but a member of an alien race who *becomes*, at the moment of speaking the ritual words, an Indian. The first time, the speaker is a Negro slave, on the run, through the whole course of a story called "Red Leaves," because he is unwilling to be killed and sent to accompany his dead master, the Chickasaw Chief, Issetibbeha. But exhausted at long last, he welcomes the fatal bite of a cottonmouth: " 'Olé, Grandfather,' the Negro said. He touched its head and watched it slash him again across the arm. . . ."

The second time, the speaker is a White man who has denied his White heritage, that Southern *alter ego* of Thoreau, Isaac McCaslin, in the much admired story "The Bear." Only after the tale is almost completely told—the bear who gives it its title dead, along with the hound, Lion, who ran it down, and the half-Indian, half-Negro Sam Fathers, who first inducted Isaac into the wilderness—does Isaac confront the snake in whom the primeval allure and horror of all three is reembodied:

> . . . the old one, the ancient and accursed about the earth, fatal and solitary . . . evocative of all knowledge and of pariah-hood and of death. At last it moved. Not the head. The elevation of the head did not change as it began to glide away from him . . . he could not quite believe that shift and flow of shadow behind that walking head could have been one snake: going and then gone; he put the other foot down at last and didn't know it, standing with one hand raised as Sam had stood that afternoon six years ago when Sam had led him into the wilderness and showed him and he ceased to be a child, speaking the old tongue which Sam had spoken that day without premeditation either: "Chief," he said, "Grandfather."

In Fenimore Cooper, the indentification of Indian and Serpent is made even closer, since the name of Natty's lifelong companion, Chingachgook, means the Great Serpent. "Now I'm naturally avarse to sarpants and I hate even the word . . . from human nature," Cooper has Natty declare, "on account of a certain sarpant at the creation of the 'arth, that outwitted the first woman; yet ever since Chingachgook earned the title he bears, why the sound is as pleasant to me as the whistle of the whip-poor-will of a calm evening." The fatal phrase is there: "outwitted the first woman"; and no Christian reader can come upon it without remembering the scriptural verse addressed to the serpent: "And I will put enmity between thee and the woman, and between thy seed and her seed. . . ." But Natty is no longer of the seed of woman, being the first (after Henry) of those Americans reborn in their encounter with the Indian on his own home grounds, which is to say, born again out of a union between men. Though he has, as he likes to boast over and over, "no cross in my blood," no taint of miscegenation in his begetting, he is neither a White Man nor a Red, but something new under the sun, the archetypal Westerner whose legend is the essential myth of America, in which the stories of Wawatam and Hannah Duston and Rip Van Winkle fuse into one.

Henry and Natty and Rip together constitute the image of the runaway from home and civilization whom we long to be when we are our most authentic selves; Dame Van Winkle and Hannah and Eve add up to the image of his dearest enemy, spokesman for the culture and the European inheritance he flees; Wawatam and Bampico and Chingachgook and the Old Serpent himself make up the Good Companion, representative of an alternative past embracing which he can achieve a future available to no European. Yet it is a melancholy myth the three define, for all its hopefulness; since the Indian, midwife and mother to the New Son whose father is his Old World self, dies giving birth—"vanishes" without a surviving bodily heir in order to leave room for his spiritual offspring. And this aspect of the mythological truth about us, Cooper knew, too, writing *The Last of the Mohicans*, whose closing pages contain in the oration of Tamenund an explicit statement of what the title implies, a revelation that the Good Companion is also the Vanishing American:

> "It is enough!" he said. "Go, children of the Lenape; the anger of Manito is not done. Why should Tamenund stay? The pale-faces are masters of the earth, and the time of the red-men has not come again. My day has been too long. In the morning I saw the sons of Unamis happy and strong; and yet, before the night has come, have I lived to see the last warrior of the wise race of the Mohicans."

But it is a dangerous myth, too, this most compelling of our archetypes, blasphemy to all who believe in the legend of Pocahontas, since it excludes and denies all that centuries of pious women have read into the lie of Captain John Smith: the vision of an Indian maiden Christianized and bleached out, her color and the concupiscence of her White lover simultaneously redeemed by Holy Matrimony. Yet it is one to which our greatest writers have compulsively returned, telling over and over again the story of that sacred-heathen love between White man and colored man in a world without women, the love which Thoreau described as "almost bare and leafless, yet not blossomless nor fruitless. . . ."

It is only a dream, perhaps, this vision of love and reconciliation between the races whose actual history is oppression and hate; but it is a dream we do not willingly surrender, our dearest myth, sustained by the faith Thoreau himself expresses at the end of the chapter in which he recounts the legend of Henry and Wawatam: "But in my dream ideal justice was at length done . . . and I was unspeakably soothed and rejoiced . . . because in dreams we never deceive ourselves, nor are deceived. . . . Our truest life is when we are in dreams awake."

THE FAILURE
OF THE WAKING DREAM

DESPITE THOREAU's waking dream, no "great poem" of the encounter with the Indian ever emerged in America—not, at least, until Wawatam-Bampico had learned to put on the disguise of a Polynesian or a Negro; and by then, the savage had been evicted from the Forest, first explored in wonder by Columbus, and sent to sea: back to the world of water which, as late as Dante, Europe had imagined the only possible West. Ishmael confronts Queequeg on the great Ocean itself; Huck confronts Jim on the Mississippi, which bears them despite themselves seaward; even Melville's occasional undisguised Indians—the Tashtego of *Moby Dick* or the "puny" half-breed squaw who accompanies the Western "giant" in *The Confidence Man*—are compelled to sail in the White man's ships, along with monomaniac whale-hunters and Indian-haters. Hawthorne, to be sure, returns over and over to the virgin wilderness, where occasionally a shadowy Redskin can be seen; but to him the American woods are "unredeemed" and demonic —"cheerful as the smile of the Great Spirit" only to the utterly damned.

As a matter of fact, Hawthorne's *Scarlet Letter* contains a rejection of the West quite as orthodox and considerably less ambivalent than Dante's own disavowal in the Ulysses Canto of the *Inferno*. "Whither leads yonder forest-track?" Hester Prynne asks her minister-lover, trying to tempt him into the westward flight, to make a real American of him. "Deeper it goes, and deeper, into the wilderness, less plainly to be seen at every step, until, some few miles hence, the yellow leaves will show no vestige of the white man's tread. There thou art free! . . . Is there not shade enough in all this boundless forest to hide thy heart from the gaze of Roger Chillingworth?" But to her hopeful query, Dimmesdale can only answer, like a good European, "Yes, Hester; but only under the fallen leaves!"—since for him the Way West is a forbidden way, leading nowhere except to death.

Among our classic writers, only Fenimore Cooper made a major effort at creating art out of the basic myths of American life. But Cooper disconcertingly condemned his own kind of fiction to extinction by predicting the disappearance of the "New Man"—that backwoods American neither Red nor White represented by his Natty Bumppo—along with that of the Indian himself.

"When I am gone," Natty says in the last of the Leatherstocking Tales, *The Prairie*, "there will be an end of my race." The word "race" is ambiguous, but there is no doubt that for Cooper he, like Chingachgook, was a Vanishing American—disappearing from our literature as well as our life, and therefore taking any possibility of other Westerns into the sunset with him.

Cooper's status is at the moment shaky in the extreme: a writer demoted by adults to the children's departments of libraries, and there unread by children who would, if they could, doubtless ship him back to the adult shelves again. Yet he is the most mythopoeically gifted of all American writers, though only, to be sure, when he touches authentic and archetypal Western material in the handful of his forty-odd books which deal with Natty Bumppo and Chingachgook. We tend to regard him condescendingly precisely for the talent he shares (the gift which has nothing to do with culture or even writing skills as traditionally understood) with certain authors of dime novels and drugstore-rack paperbacks, Zane Grey, for instance, or Clarence Faust. In his own time, however, Cooper was taken quite as seriously as his European opposite numbers, Scott and Manzoni. Only the sort of snobbism prompted by Henry James, confirmed by T. S. Eliot and academicized by F. R. Leavis, learned to regard the historical romance in general as *infra dig* and its Western form in particular as beneath contempt.

This aberration of taste had to await the twentieth century for its full development. In the American nineteenth century, writers now preferred by established critics—Hawthorne and Melville, for example—had kind things to say about Cooper, whom only a self-advertised lowbrow like Mark Twain dared publicly despise along with his peer and model, Sir Walter Scott. As a matter of fact, it is precisely for his highfalutin pretentiousness, his claim, recognized by the academic critics of the later nineteenth century, to have produced works of "Art," that Twain pretends to despise Cooper. He prefixes to his undeservedly famous essay, "Fenimore Cooper's Literary Offenses," a quotation, whose author he carefully identifies as "Prof. Lounsbury," beginning with the assertion, "*The Pathfinder* and *The Deerslayer* stand at the head of Cooper's novels as artistic creations," and ending even more unreservedly, "They were pure works of art." Then, after what he clearly takes to be a damning bill of particulars in rebuttal of the good Prof, Twain himself concludes: "A work of art? It has no invention, it has no order, system, or result; it has no life-likeness, no thrill, no stir, no seeming of reality. . . . Counting these out, what is left is Art. I think we must all admit that."

There is finally something disingenuous about his attack since it is only secondarily Cooper's good critical press and "poor English" which annoy him. What primarily irks him is "Cooper's Indians," which is to say, Cooper's mythology of the Indian, especially (what he affects not even to notice) the woodland romance between the White Man and the Indian, so central to the *Leatherstocking Tales*. Twain is, by instinct and conviction, an absolute Indian hater, consumed by the desire to destroy not merely real Indians, but any image of Indian life which stands between White Americans and a total commitment to genocide. His only notable Indian character is Injun Joe, that haunter of caves and hater of white females, who stalks the underground darkness of *Tom Sawyer* and is finally imagined dying the most dreadful of deaths—at the barred gate which would have let him back into the daylight world of Aunt Polly and Becky Thatcher.

Twain was, as a matter of fact, obsessed by a hatred of Indians from the very beginning of his literary career—evoking them, quite unexpectedly and with embarrassing fury, for instance, as he stands on the shores of Lake Como during that tourist expedition to the Old World recounted in *Innocents Abroad*. Confronted with the alien beauty of Europe, Twain staunchly asserts the superiority of the American landscape, especially Lake Tahoe; but once he has returned to the American West in his imagination, he is overtaken by the never-quite-subdued hostility so inextricably bound up with that region for him:

> Tahoe means grasshoppers. It means grasshopper soup. It is Indian and suggestive of Indians. They say it is Paiute—possibly it is Digger. I am satisfied it was named by the Diggers—those degraded savages who roast their dead relatives, then mix the human grease and ashes of bone with tar and "gaum" it thick all over their heads and foreheads and ears, and go caterwauling about the hills and call it *mourning. These* are the gentry that named the lake.
>
> People say that Tahoe means "silver lake"—"limpid water"—"falling leaf." Bosh. It means grasshopper soup, the favorite dish of the Digger tribe—and of the Paiutes as well. It isn't worthwhile, in these practical times, for people to talk about Indian poetry—there never was any in them—except in the Fenimore Cooper Indians. But *they* are an extinct tribe that never existed. I know the Noble Red Man. I have camped with the Indians; I have been on the warpath with them—for grasshoppers; helped them steal cattle; I have roamed

with them, scalped them, had them for breakfast. I would gladly eat the whole race if I had a chance.

It is astonishing self-betrayal, more revelatory certainly about Twain's anti-Cooperism and its deep sources than the critical essay devoted to Cooper; and it evokes in the minds of latter-day readers the twenty-sixth chapter of Melville's *The Confidence Man*, "Containing the metaphysics of Indian Hating, according to the views of one evidently not so prepossessed as Rousseau in favor of Savages"—which Twain quite probably never read, but which nonetheless serves as a gloss to his meditations beside Lake Como.

It is hard to know how Melville himself stood on the subject of Indian-hating, since he does not speak to us in his own editorial voice but presents instead the views of a fictional spokesman, purportedly quoting a certain Judge James Hall on the exploits of the famed Indian Killer, Colonel John Moredock, in order to answer the question: "Why the backwoodsman still regards the red man in much the same spirit that a jury does a murderer, or a trapper a wild cat." "*The* backwoodsman," Melville's mouthpiece says, as if Indian-lovers had never existed in the woods, no Alexander Henry in fact, no Natty Bumppo in fiction—only what he calls the "Leather-Stocking Nemesis," pledged to a campaign of extermination against "Indian lying, Indian theft, Indian double-dealing, Indian fraud and perfidy, Indian want of conscience, Indian bloodthirstiness, Indian diabolism." It is this kind of backwoodsman, at any rate, whom he eulogizes as representing "to America what Alexander was to Asia—Captain in the vanguard of a conquering civilization. . . . The tide of emigration, let it roll as it will, never overwhelms the backwoodsman into itself; he rides upon the advance, as the Polynesian upon the comb of the surf. Thus though he keep moving on through life, he maintains with respect to nature much the same unaltered relation throughout; with her creatures, too, including panthers and Indians."

With such wary and murderous Westerners, at any rate, Twain identified himself—however much they may have looked at him as an alien and tenderfoot when he penetrated their territory—since he knew enough of their literature and conversation to feel that, like himself, all true Indian haters were true lovers of their White Mothers: defenders of those whom their own fathers had proved too weak to protect. Typically, the Indian Killer begins his career with an act of vengeance for a murdered mother, only to become addicted to bloodshed, or, perhaps, convinced that as long as a single Redskin survives, some paleface Mama is in danger of death or worse. It is not unlikely, in fact, that, whatever his ignorance of Melville, Twain may have read Judge Hall's original chronicle of Colonel Moredock, reprinted a score of times in periodicals and books:

> John Moredock was the son of a woman who was married several times, and was as often widowed by the tomahawk of the savage. . . . She was at last induced to join a party about to remove to Illinois. . . . Mrs. Moredock and her friends . . . proceeded in safety until they reached the Grand Tower of the Mississippi, where . . . it became necessary for the boatman to land. . . . Here a party of Indians, lying in wait, rushed upon them, and murdered the whole party. Mrs. Moredock was among the victims, and *all* her children, except John. . . .
>
> . . . He resolved upon executing vengeance, and immediately took measures to discover the actual perpetrators of the massacre. It was ascertained that the outrage was committed by a party of twenty or thirty Indians. . . . Shortly after, he . . . had the good fortune to discover them one evening, on an island. . . . Three of the Indians escaped . . . while the whites lost not a man.
>
> But Moredock was not satisfied while one of the murderers of his mother remained. He learned to rec-

ognize the names and persons of the three that had escaped, and these he pursued in secret, but untiring diligence, until they all fell by his own hand. Nor was he yet satisfied. He had become a hunter and warrior . . . . . He had resolved never to spare an Indian, and though he made no boast of this determination, and seldom avowed it, it became the ruling passion of his life. . . . He thought it praiseworthy to kill an Indian; and would roam through the forest silently and alone, for days and weeks, with this single purpose. . . . He died four years ago, an old man, and it is supposed never in his life failed to embrace an opportunity to kill a savage.

Certainly Twain takes the grim opinion of Redskin nature maintained by such bloodthirsty defenders of mother as a necessary antidote to Cooper's implicitly antifeminist idealizations. Yet he could never quite stay away from Cooper's themes; and, in fact, they haunt *Huckleberry Finn*, which, running its narrative course southward along the Mississippi, that natural and mythological boundary between East and West, cannot help defining the place where the Western properly begins for late nineteenth century America. Though Jim is introduced in Hannibal itself as a satisfactorily Southern darky, once on the river, he yearns to become an Indian, a Good Companion on the model of Wawatam or Chingachgook. And, on the raft and in the nighttime, he momentarily achieves that archetypal transformation; but first Huck, then Tom, intervenes (which is to say, Twain's timid second thoughts, and timider third ones), forcing the action into a world of mountain feuds, lynch mobs, rewards for fugitive slaves, pretensions to the values of aristocratic Europe, and good home cooking down on the farm—in short, to the mythic South, where he must become Jim Crow once more and perform travesties of his own suffering to keep us laughing.

At the very end of the book, however, Twain promises the reader a sequel in which Huck and Jim and Tom would make it into the real—the non-Southern—West at last, by lighting out for the Territory, and "howling adventures amongst the Injuns." That sequel Twain actually began, wrestled with, at last abandoned unfinished; and though what remains of it has not yet seen the light, apparently the manuscript, which Twain himself finally considered a "bore," is about to be published: a burlesque of Cooper, we are assured by its editors, but by that very token, we can surmise, an inverted tribute to him.

Edgar Allan Poe, too, tried unsuccessfully to write a Western; an anomalous attempt, it seems at first glance, on the part of an author committed chiefly to producing the culturally pretentious kind of Southern in which certain melodramatic effects destined to become standard in the genre were played out against pseudo-European backgrounds. It is tempting to dismiss his effort as merely one more instance of his *other* kind of story: the travesty-hoax, of which he was as fond as Mark Twain himself, and to which he turned whenever he yearned to be funny rather than horrific, commercial rather than artistic—thus mocking not only his own inflated ambitions, but also the gullibility of his provincial audience.

There seems little doubt, at any rate, that he dreamed of making money for a change by exploiting what he had come to believe was an inevitably best-selling form of the novel. Even three years after he had abandoned his single attempt at a "Western," he was still teasing himself with these possibilities, though with a confirmed sense that they were not for him, as he sat down in 1843 to review Cooper's *Wyandotté*.

From the little known Indian novel before him, Poe passed quickly to a consideration of the Leatherstocking Tales and their phenomenal success. ". . . we mean to suggest," he writes somewhat mournfully, "that this theme—life in the Wilderness—is one of intrinsic and universal interest . . . a theme, like that of life upon the ocean, so unfailingly omniprevalent in its power of arresting and absorbing attention, that . . . success or popularity is, with such a subject, expected as a matter of course. . . ."

He is very close here to grasping the mythic nature of the Western; but aspirations to High culture get in his way. He hastens to add that the "man of genius . . . more interested in fame than popularity," i.e., the sort of "true artist" he liked to fancy himself, must avoid such themes at all costs; for the works which embody them belong to what he calls the "popular division" of fiction—and are, therefore, soon "lost or forgotten; or remembered, if at all, with something very nearly akin to contempt."

But surely his eagerness to classify himself with Brockden Brown and John Neal and Hawthorne rather than Fenimore Cooper arises from the fact that he had *already* tried and failed at a Cooper-like tale of "life in the Wilderness." Perhaps his mistake had been not emulating that "popular" master directly enough, but turning for a model instead to the *Journals* of Lewis and Clark, which belong to history rather than myth. Certainly, his *Journal of Julius Rodman* is only the first in a series of unsuccessful attempts to make literature of those intriguing but somehow fictionally intractable documents—attempts which have continued down to the verge of our own time in Robert Penn Warren's *Brother to Dragons,* for instance, and a novel by the indefatigable Vardis Fisher.

For Poe the choice was almost inevitable, however, Virginian that he remained in his deepest self-consciousness (despite an effort to identify himself as a "Bostonian" on the title page of his first published volume of verse), since the expedition that opened the ultimate West was the work of Virginians, an offshoot, as it were, of the history of that state. Meriwether Lewis was a Virginian, as was his associate Clark, and Thomas Jefferson, his sponsor and friend, who, having long dreamed the world Lewis was to walk, made the venture possible. From our first American West, the West of John Smith and Pocahontas, came the men who achieved the last—crying out with just such joy when they reached the shores on which our West ends as those earliest explorers had felt reaching those beaches where it all began. How appropriate it would have been, finally, had a Virginian then turned their adventure and their passion into a prose epic as moving as *Moby Dick*. But, despite his antecedents, Poe could not bring it off; and his failure is instructive not only in regard to his own limitations, but to those of the genre as well—at least from his time on.

In him, at any rate, one source of confusion is a hopeless jumbling together of the Southern and the Western, to the detriment of both. Perhaps this is inevitable, given the notion—implicit in the double status of Virginia as the heartland of Southern chivalry and the place of our first encounter with the Indian—that mythological South and mythological West constitute a single archetypal region, a unified anti-Northeast. With this hybrid region, certainly, Poe identified his fate as a writer, as Edwin Fussell quite convincingly demonstrates in his otherwise reasonably unconvincing study, *Frontier: American Literature and the American West*. Throughout his life, Poe wrote letters referring to his "warm friends . . . in the South and West" who would redeem him from the neglect of the North and East; and he was forever laying plans, which never quite materialized, "to go South and West, among my personal and literary friends. . . ."

Always it is South *and* West, away from the older cities and their closed cultural world, to a bi-directional elsewhere of open possibility. But whatever the merits of such a view for understanding the nature of the American audience, it proved as negative an influence on the development of the Western after the time of Cooper as Cooper's own vision of the extinction of his protagonists. In light of this, however, we can understand at least why Poe provides Gordon Pym, the hero of his first romance of "life in the wilderness," with an account of the opening of the West, though Pym is heading *South* as far as the Pole. If South and West are one, what more appropriate reading matter on an antarctic voyage than the chronicles of "the expedition of Lewis and Clark to the mouth of the Columbia"?

And what more appropriate traveling companion and guide for Pym than the half-breed Indian Dirk Peters, ". . . the son of an Indian woman of the tribe of the Upsarokas, who live among the fastnesses of the Black Hills, near the source of the Missouri." But this takes us back, of course, to the jumping-off place of Lewis and Clark, a home country which, along with Peters' race, gives assurance of his friendliness, despite the bald head, bowed legs, and long protruding teeth that lend him the aspect more of an ogre than of a man. It is as if Poe were trying to reimagine, in a watery and icy South, the Western forest-romance lived by Alexander Henry and redreamed by James Fenimore Cooper.

As the shipmates, White and Red, move closer and closer to the White World of the South Pole, the water and air begin disconcertingly to grow warmer and warmer around them; and the inhabitants of an antarctic island on which they beach turn out to be a strange and surly breed of super-Negroes—whose very teeth are black. This is no longer any West we can acknowledge. We have, in fact, been carried back—along with Pym and Peters, who think they have embarked on a voyage of exploration but are riding really the currents of a Poe nightmare—into "Old Virginny." But this is a world in which Red no longer has an archetypal place; so we are not surprised when Pym's half-breed companion, fleeing the assaults of the Blacks along with his friend, turns *White*.

"We alone had escaped from the tempest of that overwhelming destruction," Poe writes of the pair, after the rest of the crew have been destroyed by the treacherous natives; then forgetting Peters' Indian mother completely, "We are the only living white men upon the island." And it does not matter that afterward, when Poe's hero is restored to life in the arms of his wild comrade, Poe tries to make that comrade a colored man once more: "a dusky, fiendish, and filmy figure stood immediately beneath me; and, sighing, I sunk down with a bursting heart, and plunged within its arms. I had swooned, and Peters caught me as I fell . . . I felt a new being. . . ." Even the images of orgasm and rebirth do not help, yet it is as close as Poe is ever to come to the essential Western myth of male companionship triumphing over hostility between the races and death itself.

In Poe's final attempt at a "wilderness" fiction, *The Journal of Julius Rodman,* he provides *no* Indian companion, male or female, for his White protagonist, though the scene is actually the American West this time, and his inspiration came from the diaries of Lewis and Clark, in which at least Sacajawea, that Pocahontas on horseback, was available as a model. Julius' only real companion is White, and Southern to boot, one "Andrew Thornton, also a Virginian," of whom he is represented as saying, "Thornton was precisely the kind of individual to whom I could unburthen my full heart. . . . We were as intimate . . . as brothers could possibly be. . . ." Julius himself is only *finally* a Virginian, having been born in New York and come South rather late in life; but other members of the expedition besides Thornton belong by birthright to the Old Dominion, as is appropriate to a fictional band whom Poe thinks of as competing with their historical Virginian counterparts on all fronts.

Poe himself was a Virginian only by adoption, after all, and his Julius Rodman—though he may have crossed the Rockies, as Poe boasts, "prior to the expedition of Lewis and Clark"—is in many respects more like Poe than like Meriwether Lewis. Nonetheless the landscape through which Rodman makes his way, as well as the adventures he endures, are all borrowed from his fellow Virginian, whose facts Poe used to eke out his own baffled invention. Yet what Poe so ungraciously borrowed, he also drastically altered in tone, turning the cool observations of Meriwether Lewis, his elegant and spare Western style, into a kind of melancholy poetry more congenial to the melodramatic Southern, the creation of which was Poe's great triumph. Boasting of their author's superiority to his historical opposite number, Poe's imaginary editors tell us that what distinguishes Rodman's account is "a vast deal of romantic fervor, very different from the lukewarm and statistical air which pervades most records of this kind. . . ." And they even confess, with a great show of objectivity, that, though ever more scrupulous in matters of fact than Lewis, ". . . in all points which relate to effects, on the contrary, Mr. Rodman's peculiar temperament leads him into excess."

What that "peculiar temperament" is, the editors explain in their pseudo-introduction to Rodman's *Journal,* applying the term "hereditary hypochondriac" to the swarthy and oddly semitic *alter ego* of Poe who usurps the place of Lewis, Jefferson's blue-eyed foster son. "Short in stature," the description of Rodman runs, "not being more than five feet three or four inches high . . . with legs somewhat bowed. His physiognomy of Jewish cast, his lips thin, and his complexion saturnine." And reading further, we learn that "He was possessed with a burning love of nature; and worshipped her, perhaps, more in her drear and savage aspects, than in her manifestations of placidity and joy."

It is, then, a deliberately Gothicized nature with which we are presented by Poe, a wilderness bathed in the black light of what was once called the "Dark Sublime"; but despite its triumphs on all other topological fronts, North and East as well as South, the Gothic mode somehow will not do for the Western. And it is especially out of key in retelling the tale of an expedition which marked its arrival on the shores of the Pacific with the journal entry: "Great joy in camp. . . ."

There may well have lurked somewhere in Lewis feelings darker than the "great joy" he chose to celebrate; but he betrayed them only once, in the meditations he set down on his thirty-first birthday, confessing over a campfire: "I viewed with regret the many hours I have spent in indolence . . ." In a moment, however, he seemed to have recovered, writing "I dash from me the gloomy thought..." and rising to continue his successful adventure.

Still—as Poe knew and we cannot forget—he was dead less than five years later, drunken surely and in despair: the victim, it used to be thought, of his own hand, though these days some historians incline to believe that he was murdered at a seedy way-station on the Natchez Trace called Grinder's Stand. Certainly, Jefferson considered that death a suicide, remarking with barely concealed dismay: "He was much afflicted and habitually so, with hypochondria. This was probably increased by the habit into which he had fallen and the painful reflections that would necessarily produce in a mind like his." And it is Jefferson's Lewis, caught between melancholy and the *mania a potu* (as Poe was accustomed elegantly to put it), that the third Virginian must have found especially sympathetic.

But the Lewis of the *Journals* is neither melancholy nor alcoholic, though it is hard finally to find an epithet for the mind behind those documents—so festive, so joyfully erotic, so nearly *comic,* in the highest and driest sense of the word. It is not the death of his European consciousness that Lewis seems to be pursuing—as Poe would have us believe of Rodman—but a mating of his consciousness to whatever it is the wilderness represents. And though there is much grief involved in the long passage to the Pacific, quite often all the real danger, discomfort, and disease disappears in the celebration of that mating. In the journal entry for more than one night, we read of Lewis falling asleep with the noise of singing and dancing in his ears, his men and the Indians cavorting together.

And even the consequences of that union, the venereal affliction which dogged his amorous expedition, did not long dismay him. In every Indian camp, he inquired hopefully about specific remedies for the diseases of love, being a man who believed in cures, solutions, reconciliations: a true spokesman for the cool and rational optimism of Jefferson, and, therefore, the potential source of the blithe Western, which even Cooper (obsessed by the vision of vanishing races) could not quite write. Certainly Lewis was—having really become a Westerner—utterly alien to the spirit of the crypto-Southern which Poe tried to write.

The absence of Sacajawea in Poe indicates the absence of much else that is essential to Lewis' account, as encounters with grizzlies and war parties and illness are not; but for the *eros* of the *Journals,* Poe has as little use as for the *eros* of *The Last of the Mohicans.* He wants to chill our blood rather than stir our loins, warm our hearts, or reassure our heads; consequently he exploits only what is horrific or "drear" in Lewis and Clark: the desolate scenery, the ferocious beasts, and the already half-mythologized Sioux.

Nothing quite terrible enough to satisfy the Gothic imagination actually occurred on the expedition, however, and so Poe is driven to exaggerate the dangers he borrows from the original account. Yet conviction keeps failing him; and in the scene on which he petered out, involving a brush with a pair of brown bears on the edge of a cliff, he lets all tension dissolve at the critical point, falling away into the most perfunctory sort of rescue: "we heard a shot, and the huge beast fell at our feet, just when we felt his hot and horribly fetid breath in our faces. . . ." Obviously, he had lost faith in what he was doing; he was unable to scare himself, much less his readers, as he longed always to do.

The real West, alas, contains no horrors which correspond to the Southerner's deep nightmare terrors. For Poe, even the Sioux will not work, though he tries hard to extort a shudder from their grotesque appearance: "an ugly ill-made race . . . their eyes protruding and dull . . . the whole surface of the body is painted with grease and coal. . . ." They are only *painted* black, however; and to Poe only the Negro adequately represents the blackness of darkness, and the Negro does not belong to the West. To be sure, Clark had actually brought his slave York with him on the expedition—presumably not only for service, but out of the kind of nostalgia for the familiar that had induced Lewis to take his favorite dog. But York is everywhere in the

Journals a source not of horror, but of somewhat condescending humor: funny even in his minor mishaps (he seems to have frozen his penis, for instance, on one particularly cold day), but especially because of his amorous conquests among the Indians, and their constant incredulity before his color.

At this point in their history, the savages had come to terms with White and Red, the color of their invaders and their own, of which they had not even been aware until the moment of invasion; but Black seemed to them one color too many, quite outside the human spectrum. And sensing this, York seems to have found pleasure in putting them on: "All flocked about him and examined him from top to toe, he carried on the joke and made himself more turribil than we wished him to doe." There is, in fact, something which not merely excites laughter but teases the imagination in this first comic encounter of the two colored races, in whose presence White ex-Europeans have had to play out their destiny in America: the enslaved Black Man, destined to be freed to subtler indignities, as York himself was freed after the return; and the free Red Man, destined to enslavement without even the name that makes protest possible. Indeed, the figure of York has intrigued recent novelists, who have imagined his descendants surviving into the New West: Lavender, for instance, in Thomas Berger's *Little Big Man*, and Ned York in my own "The First Spade in the West."

Though willing to play the clown, and even on occasion dance a jig, York was by no means just a buffoon, but a man proud of his strength and potency, given his vote with all the rest at moments of decision. Poe, however, to whom the Negro has to be Sambo if he is not a Black terrorist, degrades and caricatures him as Toby, turning him into an old duffer for a start, and making him as unbeautiful as possible besides: "Toby, moreover, was as ugly an old gentleman as ever spoke, having all the peculiar features of his race—the swollen lips, large white protruding eyes, flat nose, long ears, pot-belly, and bow-legs." And when, standing stark naked before them, Toby lets the Assiniboines touch "the wool on his head" and rub his skin with spit, then performs his famous jig, Poe tells us, in an ironic deprecation: "wonder was now at its height. Approbation could go no further." But we are watching a Wild West show no longer, only a minstrel show in the nude.

For all its nudity, however, it remains without sex, since for Poe to Southernize means to bowdlerize—the time of Faulknerian frankness lying still far ahead. He will not even tell us, as his fellow Southerner, Robert Penn Warren, is to do in *Brother to Dragons* more than a hundred years later, of Lewis' "good nigger York, who left his seed in every tribe across the continent. . . ."

Warren's Gothicized sex, however, comes no closer than Poe's Gothic sexlessness to Lewis' dispassionate comment on the coupling of White men and Red women in the Western wilderness; to Warren the coupling of Indians as observed by Lewis is translated into ". . . the reek of sour bodies and the pathos of the bestial face," causing "nausea . . . in your gut, even as, for sympathy, your parts twisted. . . ." But Lewis's customary tone is detached, indulgent, mildly mocking:

> I have requested the men to give them [certain Indian husbands] no cause of jelousy by having connection with their women without their knowledge . . . to prevent the mutual exchange of good office altogether I know it is impossible to effect; particularly on the part of our young men whom some months of abstinence have made very polite to these tawny damsels.

The desexing of the West (with the consequent loss of a chief possibility of humor in the genre) is of critical importance in the deposition of the Western from the center to the periphery of our literature. Certainly, the de-crabbed, castrated Westerner, that clean, toe-twisting, hat-tipping White Knight embodied finally in Gary Cooper, betrays the truth of American history; and an attempt, like Poe's, to recount the opening of the trans-Mississippi West without passion and venereal disease is an unintentional travesty. Nonetheless, sexual candor alone cannot redeem the veracity and power of the form, as Warren's tortured anti-Western sufficiently testifies.

Even a writer completely Western in origin and aspiration, like A. B. Guthrie, can come to grief in a similar way. His *The Big Sky* attempts to break through the stereotypes of the popular Western by revealing the not-very-well-kept secret that even Mountain Men in pioneering times occasionally got gonorrhea: a fact which the children's version of his book (it is a sign of the place to which the Western had fallen, that one followed almost immediately) quite properly conceals. Disconcertingly, however, the expurgated version moves us just as much and as little as the original—which seems in consequence something of a hoax: a juvenile disguised as adult fare by a certain amount of frankness about sex.

The illusion of realism leads in the Western merely from one level of sentimentality to another, from the sort of lies men used to tell one another in the presence of ladies to the sort of half-truths they used to exchange when those ladies were absent: like smoking car stories with western settings; or such drawings as the well-known pair by the cowboy artist Charlie Russell showing a cowpuncher before and after his visit to the local whorehouse—over the title, *A Little Bit of Pleasure, A Little Bit of Pain, A Little Bit of Sunshine, A Little Bit of Rain*.

Those more sophisticated recent pop novels which play off, for the laughs, the seamier side of Western history against its sentimental expurgations are not quite satisfactory either. Yet to understand the West as somehow a joke comes a little closer to getting it straight; and there is a reward more substantial than the mere pleasures of muckraking in learning that one or another of those lantern-jawed gunslingers celebrated on TV was in fact a "pimp-fighter," bringing whores into the Territory and living on them thereafter. But the tension between the fact and the legend of Pocahontas-Sacajawea is a clue only to the comic limits of the Western myth; for some indication of where its real center lies, we must look further and deeper. Fenimore Cooper himself, for instance, is impossibly reticent on the score of sex, but seems authentic and moving all the same; for in the *Leatherstocking Tales*, though passion and its melancholy aftermath are expurgated, the myth of the Good Companions in the Woods remains.

Only when this myth goes is the Western deprived of its essential power: when chivalry à la Sir Walter Scott replaces the dream of Wawatam, and the Westerner comes to be portrayed as an Ivanhoe in chaps: i.e., one who does not flee the good White woman at home, but rather risks his life to defend her against the forces of savagery. All the hero of the southernized Western asks of that good woman in return is that she recognize the legitimacy of the means by which he makes her existence safe, and give up any vestigial Christian scruples against the use of violence.

The pattern is set once and for all in Owen Wister's *The Virginian*, once taught in high school classrooms side by side with its English prototype, *Ivanhoe*, since it asks to be accepted as *belles-lettres* rather than mere entertainment, like those shabby dime novels which fill the decades between it and the *Leatherstocking Tales*. But the very title of Wister's novel, completed appropriately enough in Charleston, South Carolina, in 1902, though set in Wyoming "between 1874 and 1890," declares the values of his hero—the so-called Code of the West—the very same which set in motion those other White Knights of the time, the Ku Klux Klan. And just as apologists for the latter present them as defending their women against the broken promises of politicians in the Northeast and the savage lust of Black Men at home, so Wister speaks of "the horseman, the cow-puncher, the last romantic figure upon our soil" as upholding standards of behavior long lapsed, not only for the renegade on the Western frontier, but for the overcivilized in the polite centers of the North and East. "If he gave his word, he kept it; Wall Street would have found him behind the times. Nor did he talk lewdly to women; Newport would have found him old-fashioned."

But behind the talk of honesty and chivalry, it is personal violence, taking the law into one's own hands, for which *The Virginian*—along with all of its recastings and imitations right down to *High Noon*—apologizes. The duel and the lynching represent its notions of honor and glory; and images of these have occupied the center of the genteel or *kitsch* Western ever since, in pulp magazines, in hardcover or paperback books, on radio, TV, or in the movies: the posse riding in a cloud of dust toward the moment of the kill, or the defender of the good tottering on his high heels down some dusty, abandoned street between false storefronts, his hand hovering just above the butt of his six-shooter. It hardly matters, band of vigilantes against band of outlaws or single champion against single villain—the meaning is the same: a plea for extra-legal violence as the sole bastion of true justice in a world where authority is corrupt and savagery ever ready to explode. And it is, perhaps, quite as much a product of the reaction against Reconstruction as those novels of Thomas Dixon, Jr., *The Leopard's Spots* and *The Clansman,* from which D. W. Griffith made *The Birth of a Nation.* Like Dixon, at any rate, Wister seems in retrospect only a preparation for films to follow—a storehouse of fantasies to be indulged in the communal loneliness of the darkened movie palace, after the Old West like the Old South was good and dead.

And just as Dixon's fictions were an imaginative, almost a mythological, justification for the oppression of the Negro, so those of Wister and his imitators were, though less explicitly, an analogous justification for the extermination of the Indian. The gunning down or mass pursuit of the man outside the law, the renegade, the White man turned "savage," is an analogue for genocide: the destruction of those savages to whom the West first belonged, and who insisted on remaining outside the White Man's law and order.

Sometimes actual Indians appear in the White Man's

Western, a howling mob without faces, closing in on the circle of covered wagons or heaving burning torches into the settlement; and sometimes men who have actually gone over to the Indians, betraying their own kind ("Simon Girty" was for many years the name that represented to the popular mind the "dirty renegade"), are cast in the villain's role. But the Redskins are present always by implication at least—even in the shootdown, traditionally reserved for WASPS only, when the paleface in a White Hat, beating the paleface in a Black Hat to the draw, symbolically kills the wild Indian in us all.

Such scenes aspire to the status of myth; but they are typically presented to us in a historic rather than mythic setting, taken out of the timeless archaic world which Fenimore Cooper was still able to imagine, and put into a just-vanished past, more appropriate to easy nostalgia than poetry. *When men were men and women liked it,* the customary regretful phrase goes, ambiguously suggesting that the wish-dream behind *The Virginian* could belong either to castrated man in an industrialized, urbanized world, or to the women who collaborated with the machines in their castration—and then lived to regret it. But such historicizing, sentimentalizing, and Southernizing, such a full-scale Sir Walter Scottification of the West, could not occur until the myth of the West had become a source of nostalgia rather than hope—a way of defining the Other Place rather than This Place, where we once were rather than where we go from here.

The Western had from the start been bowdlerized and sentimentalized, but never entirely falsified; Natty Bumppo was invented, after all, as a garrulous old man whose nose ran, and Chingachgook first portrayed as a hopeless drunk. Only after the Anglo-Saxon founding fathers of the White New World had given way to a generation of effete sons, who snubbed or patronized the more recent immigrants from the Mediterranean South or Slavic East of Europe, and a generation of earnest daughters, who schooled the children of those immigrants to believe that there were real men out there once in the West, was the real damage done.

At that point, no one in the East seemed any longer to remember, and no one in the actual West (just beginning to contemplate tourism as a major industry) cared to remind them, that it was gunslingers and pimps, habitual failures and refugees from law and order, as well as certain dogged pursuers of a dream, who had actually made the West—not Ivanhoes in chaps, desexed and odorless, though still lethal to cross and quick on the draw. Careful men, if violent ones, real Westerners preferred to gun their enemies down with a shotgun from behind some convenient shelter; but in fantasy they walk toward each other forever, face to face, down sun-bright streets—ready for the showdown, which is to say, the last form of chivalric duel. No wonder the myth had to be immunized against reality, more and more narrowly localized in time and space—to keep anyone from making comparisons with a world he knew at first hand.

The decade just after the Civil War becomes the mythological time, the "Far West"—Montana, Wyoming, Texas, Nevada, etc.—the mythological place in which Indians are subdued, or Mormons (anti-Mormonism being the anti-Semitism of the West), or outlaws; though the essential war is against women who, sustained by misguided ministers or spineless dandies from the East, advocate not only charity and forgiveness, but also compliance with the Law, which to the writer of Westerns seems typically a mere camouflage for villainy. Or, perhaps, Christianity is the real, the final enemy; since in the fable first worked out in *The Virginian*, religious pacifism is invariably portrayed as capitulating to lynch law and the duel. And how could it be otherwise, since the spokesman for pacifism is always a woman; and readers, whatever their sex, of that transitional Western, which dominates the scene between the time of Cooper and the Dime Novel and that of the emergence of the New Western, would not have tolerated a defeat of the male.

For a real sense of the passion involved in the moment of female capitulation to force, we must turn to the *locus classicus* in Zane Grey's *Riders of the Purple Sage*, perhaps the most popular novel of the most popular Western novelist of the first half of the twentieth century. The heroine is talking, a Mormon who has just seen the light: "Pity me —help me in my weakness. You're strong again—oh, so cruelly, coldly strong! You're killing me. . . . My master, be merciful. . . . You are a man! I never knew it till now. Some wonderful change came to me when you buckled on those guns . . . I loved you then. . . ." It is a speech quite indistinguishable from that of the heroine in Dixon's *The Leopard's Spots*, who sends out her man to found the Klan.

Small wonder, then, that when a writer of real talent and honesty appeared at last in the West, it was not an actual Western he was moved to write, but an anti-Southern in a Western landscape. Walter Van Tilburg Clark's *The Oxbow Incident* is a deeply moving novel, and it made an even more impressive motion picture; yet it is not a Western in the archetypal sense I have been trying to define. Though it is set in Nevada just after the end of the Civil War, its chief villain is an ex-Confederate General, its most important colored man a Negro rather than an Indian; and it is finally about lynching, an illustrated sermon *against* lynching this time at least. Since *The Oxbow Incident*, Clark has tried again—in a second novel, *The Track of the Cat*, for instance, and in a group of stories collected in the volume called *The Watchful Gods*. The novel is patently, almost embarrassingly, a really Big Try, a kind of *Moby Dick* removed from the South Pacific to the mountains of the West, with a fabulous totem animal who means different things to each of his hunters, and a Dark Companion for the preferred hunter—an Indian, of course, in this case —whose name, Joe Sam, suggests that Clark may also have had in mind the model of Faulkner's "The Bear."

Clark's fable is overwhelmed by its symbolism, betrayed by the example of the masters of narrative whom Clark has too oppressively in mind: Melville and Faulkner and, even, Henry James. Besides, his characters have too much inwardness for the actors in a myth, who must project, not explore, the darkness of the soul; for Clark cannot resist an interior monologue any more than he can a symbol. And this may explain why the most satisfactory of all his works is the short story "Hook," with its oddly, ironically introspective hero, the hawk. There is a special kind of pleasure, a sort of somber yet satisfactory joke, in the notion of a bird thinking, which becomes a bore when that bird is transformed into a more conventional Western hero, which is to say, a New Man. In any case, Clark himself seems to have sensed his own predicament and to have found no way to solve it, for he has lapsed into silence; checking the dates of his books, we discover, dismayed, that he has published nothing since 1950.

To be sure, there has been a movie version of *The Track of the Cat* since, recent enough to have cast Robert Mitchum as its villain; but it served only to reveal the pretentious hollowness of the book. Perhaps what will not film in a genre as myth-ridden as the Western, what refuses translation into visual images is, by that token, a failure; certainly such a conclusion is suggested by a comparison of the fate on the screen of *The Oxbow Incident* and its successor. It does not follow, however, that the success of a Western film necessarily implies the excellence of the book from which it is drawn. *Shane,* for instance, was considerably better as cinema than fiction; and even *The Hanging Tree* (benefited by the presence of Gary Cooper at his most wooden-faced and toe-twisting), though not quite first-rate itself, is superior to the story by Dorothy Johnson from which it derives.

In any case, neither the Jamesian inwardness of Clark's anti-Southern nor the symbolism of his later fiction has provided a useful model for redeeming the Western in the second half of the twentieth century. Quite another way is required, an approach and tone found, or tentatively suggested, in the Indian sections of Hemingway's *The Torrents of Spring* and the Hollywood Cowboy passages of Nathanael West's *The Day of the Locust*.

Hemingway wrote a great deal about Indians throughout his life. Sometimes he deals with them quite directly in the place where he had known them as a boy, in the yesterday's cutover West of Upper Michigan, as in short stories like "Indian Camp" and "Ten Little Indians"; sometimes he disguises them as European peasants in *For Whom the Bell Tolls*, as we have already noticed, in which he removes them to Spain, his alternative Montana. But the pathos in both is, even at best, a little old-fashioned, as in "Now I Lay Me," in which Nick Adams' Christian Scientist mother (spiritual descendant of Hannah Duston) burns his father's Indian collection; at worst, merely banal, as in Nick's evocation of the Ojibway girl, Trudy, in the nostalgic story, "Fathers and Sons."

> Could you say she did first what no one has ever done better and mention plump brown legs, flat belly, hard little breasts, well holding arms, quick searching tongue, the flat eyes, the good taste of mouth, then uncomfortably, tightly, sweetly, mostly, lovely, tightly, achingly, fully, finally, unendingly, never-endingly, never-to-endingly, suddenly ended, the great bird flown. . . . So that when you go in a place where Indians have lived you smell them gone and all the empty pain killer bottles and the flies that buzz do not kill the sweetgrass smell, the smoke smell and that other like a fresh cased marten skin. Not any jokes about them or old squaws take that away. Nor the sick sweet they get to have. Nor what they did finally. . . .

Faulkner, too, walks the line between old-fashioned sentimentality and sheer banality, but unlike his contemporary, Hemingway, he is concerned with the male Indian, foster-father, guide, and inductor, by way of the ritual of hunting, of a boy into the world without women, i.e., the West. What undercuts even so splendid a story of the type as "The

Bear," however, is Faulkner's subscription to the stereotype of the Vanishing American, into which the character of Sam Fathers (called elsewhere also Uncle Blue-Gum and Had-Two Fathers) dissolves at the moment of his death:

> He lay there—the copper-brown, almost hairless body, the old man, the wild man not even one generation from the woods, childless, kinless, peopleless. . . .

Hemingway, on the other hand, is haunted by the image of the Indian girl, whore and Pocahontas in one, who initiates the White boy sexually into manhood and the possibility of going East. But responding to that image, he becomes only a kind of soggy, or second-best, D. H. Lawrence; and it is consequently not at such moments that he provides cues for the New Western. That he only manages when he mocks Lawrence, and the aspects of himself most like Lawrence, in that extraordinary *tour de force* (tossed off in ten days, he tells us, to "cool out" between drafts of *The Sun Also Rises*), still disgracefully little read or known, *The Torrents of Spring*.

To be sure, he pretends that it is Sherwood Anderson alone who is the butt of his parody, but that should fool no one. Knowing his own earlier stories and the novel itself in the midst of composing which he paused to write his travesty, we realize that his own dearest and most absurd affectations are being held up to ridicule—especially at the book's climax, when Yogi Johnson is delivered from the impotence incurred in Europe (cured of Jake Barnes' disease, need I insist) by the appearance of a naked Indian woman in an Upper Michigan beanery:

> . . . They are all inside the beanery. Some do not see the others. Each are intent on themselves. Red men are intent on red men. White men are intent on white men or on white women. There are no red women. Are there no squaws any more? What has become of the squaws? Have we lost our squaws in America? Silently, through the door which she had opened, a squaw came

into the room. She was clad only in a pair of worn moccasins. On her back was a papoose. Beside her walked a husky dog.

"Don't look," the drummer shouted to the women at the counter. . . .

Yogi Johnson was not listening. Something had broken inside of him. Something had snapped as the squaw came into the room. He had a new feeling. A feeling he thought had been lost forever. Lost for always. Lost. Gone permanently. He knew now it was a mistake. He was all right now. . . .

And we are prepared for the happy interracial ending, his own stripping down to the buff:

North of the frozen little Northern town a couple walking side by side on the tracks. It is Yogi Johnson walking with the squaw. As they walk Yogi Johnson silently strips off his garments. One by one he strips off his garments, and casts them beside the track. In the end he is clad only in a worn pair of pump-maker shoes. Yogi Johnson, naked in the moonlight, walking North beside the squaw.

But the last word, the final joke, is from inside the whale; for following behind Yogi and watching him are those most immune to his romantic falsification, Indians themselves:

Behind them come two figures. Sharply etched in the moonlight. It is the two Indians. The two woods Indians. They stoop and gather up the garments Yogi Johnson has cast away. . . . The two Indians straighten up. They examine the garments.

"White chief snappy dresser," the tall Indian remarks. holding up an initialed shirt.

"White chief going get pretty cold," the small Indian remarks. . . .

For perhaps the first time in our literature, a kind of anti-Western Western is being written here, which begins by assuming the clichés and stereotypes of all the popular books which precede it, and aims not at redeeming but at *exploiting* them, bringing the full weight of their accumulated absurdities to bear in every casual quip. Self-conscious camp has overtaken the Western.

So, too, in *The Day of the Locust,* Nathanael West (there is already a wry note of burlesque in the last name he assumed for himself in place of Weinstein) plays the parody-game, this time not only with the movie images of the Westerner, but with those ex-real cowboys who come to play their own mythicized selves on the screen—or flock to Hollywood in the vain hope of doing so. Earle Shoop is West's special cowpoke, his face as artificial in real life as any screen could make it:

> ... He had a two-dimensional face that a talented child might have drawn with a ruler and a compass. His chin was perfectly round and his eyes, which were wide apart, were also round. His thin mouth ran at right angles to his straight, perpendicular nose. His reddish tan complexion was the same color from hairline to throat, as though washed in by an expert, and it completed his resemblance to a mechanical drawing.

With a break he might have been, could still become— maybe, maybe (it is the hope that draws him on)—Gary Cooper or John Wayne. But defeated in everything except small-time love-making with not-quite-Jean Harlowes, he must content himself with lounging before Hodges saddlery store—whose very hardware reflects the dreams of violence on which he was nurtured, and to which he hopes to appeal:

> ... In the window of this store was an enormous Mexican saddle covered with carved silver, and around it was arranged a large collection of torture instruments. Among other things there were fancy, braided quirts, spurs with great spiked wheels and double bits that looked as though they could break a horse's jaw without trouble. ...

He is in full regalia, of course, an outfit appropiate to his backdrop:

> ... He had on his ten-gallon hat and his high-heeled boots. Neatly folded over his left arm was a dark grey jacket. His shirt was navy-blue cotton with large polka dots, each the size of a dime. The sleeves of his shirt were not rolled, but pulled to the middle of his forearm and held there by a pair of fancy, rose armbands. ...

And when he is joined by two other Westerners, they begin a routine whose point is the pointless violence with which it ends.

> "Monro's makin' a new Buck Stevens," he said. "Will Ferris told me they'd use more than forty riders."
> Calvin turned and looked up at Earle.
> "Still got the piebald vest?" he asked slyly.
> "Why?"
> "It'll cinch you a job as a road agent."
> Tod understood that this was a joke of some sort because Calvin and Hink chuckled and slapped their thighs loudly while Earle frowned.

This is immediately followed by more repartee, ending with the presumably indecent riposte: "He dassint. He got caught in a sheep car with a pair of rubber boots on."

> It was another joke. Calvin and Hink slapped their thighs and laughed, but Tod could see they were waiting for something else. Earle, suddenly, without even shifting his weight, shot his foot out and kicked Calvin solidly in the rump. This was the real point of the joke. They were delighted by Earle's fury. Tod also laughed. The way Earle had gone from apathy to action without the usual transition was funny. The seriousness of his violence was even funnier.

There is an incidental Indian, too, in West's cockeyed world, where everybody plays himself badly, "a wrinkled Indian who had long hair held by a head strap around his forehead," and who wears a sandwich sign reading: TAKE BACK A SOUVENIR *from* TUTTLE'S TRADING POST. Introduced jovially as "Chief Kiss-My-Towkas," he laughs in response, then tells a joke or two of his own, crying at one point, for instance, in imitation of a current radio gag, "Vas you dere, Sharley," and showing "the black inside of his mouth, purple tongue and broken orange teeth." But even Hollywood Indians do not really interest West; only the Cowboy, last obscene descendant of Natty Bumppo, or perhaps Captain John Smith before him, is necessary to his fable, to get drunk, lay the blonde-bitch heroine, and fight the Mexican who is his rival. To travesty in full malice the Westerner, as Hemingway had already begun to travesty (despite his sentimental self) the Indian Maiden, which is to say, Pocahontas—this is West's contribution.

THE ANTI-POCAHONTAS
OF US ALL

AFTER THE ACHIEVEMENT of Hemingway and West, it is possible for young writers to treat the oldest American myth of the encounter between Whites and Indians as farce: to replace nostalgia with parody, sentimentality with mockery, polite female masochism with gross male sadism. Yet in the decades immediately following the publication of *Torrents of Spring* and *The Day of the Locust,* neither the reading public nor the critics seemed to know what to do with them; and they remained, therefore, without real consequence until the sixties—when, suddenly, we could no longer abide the prim Protestant versions of Pocahontas, or the grave and serious face of the Virginian as played by Gary Cooper. It was dusky sex queens which the age demanded, and seedy clowns in full Western regalia to act out for laughs the death of the West; it was Lee Marvin we wanted, drunken and doomed in his double comic role in *Cat Ballou,* or half beaten to death by a high-heeled shoe in the hands of a menopausal neurotic as in *Ship of Fools.*

It is in the novel, however, that the New Western properly begins, with the appearance in 1960 of John Barth's *The Sot-Weed Factor.* Barth's novel interweaves its account of the adventures of Ebenezer Cooke, first Poet Laureate of Maryland, with revelations of what *really* happened between Pocahontas and Captain John Smith. The sources for the truth about the oldest and palpably falsest of all American legends, Barth would have us believe, are *The Secret*

Historie of Smith himself, and the *Journal* of his companion, Henry Burlingame—documents which the author knows to be more reliable than the good Captain's *True Relation,* because he composed them himself. That his truth is a *naked* truth does not surprise us; for, as we have seen already, the naked Pocahontas—Indian Princess and Daughter of the Manito—has always striven to emerge from the overdressed convert of the single Renaissance portrait, which reveals nothing of her dusky flesh except the bare face above her ruff. It is with relief that we find Barth's daughter of Powhatan nude as the Indian girl in Hemingway's Petoskey beanery, under John Smith's concupiscent stare:

> In the center of his smalle ring sat the Emperour Powhatan . . . and before him, upon a manner of altar stone, lay Pocahontas, stript & trust with thongs of hyde for the heethenish rites. Yet maugre the rudeness of her position, the Princesse seem'd not a whit alarm'd, but wore an huge smyle upon her face. . . . We were fetch'd into the small circle and station'd before the altar of *Venus* (to looke whereon brought the blush to my cheeks). . . .

The impulse to strip Pocahontas to the dusky skin is variously motivated—arising sometimes out of sheer scholarship, sometimes out of the sacrilegious impulse that underlay the development of the novel from the beginnings of Realism to the emergence of Pop Art—from the moment when a form born as entertainment began to think of itself as "art," to the moment when it turned in mockery on its own pretensions.

Barth is, in this respect, our Voltaire and Anatole France rolled into one, a defiler and riddler and cutter, for whom Pocahontas is a girl "with everie indecent promise in her eyes . . . all her movements exaggerated, and none befitting any save a Drury Lane vestall. . . ." Obviously, she is intended from all time for Barth's John Smith, who "taketh inordinate pride in his virilitie . . . and boasteth to have known every kind of woman on earth in all of Aretine's positions."

At their first meeting, at any rate, he sets her to giggling lasciviously with a display of obscene pictures, and at their last, brutally deflowers her, though only with the aid of an eggplant and an aphrodisiac potion, since the Captain, according to his friend Henry Burlingame, was "for all his boasting . . . but passing well equipt for Venereal exercise." And Pocahontas (whose very name, Barth would have us believe, means "the small one") possessed "a singular physical short-coming . . . to witt: her privitie was that nice, and the tympanum therein so surpassing stout, as to render it infrangible." Nonetheless, reinforced by his secret formula, John Smith succeeds at the impossible, and escapes the death his failure would have brought upon him and his companions:

> Straight leapt my Captain to his work, whereof I can bring myself to say naught save this: Mercifull, mercifull, the Providence, that kept the heethen maid aswoon, while that my Captain did what none had done before! And so inordinatelie withal, that anon the Emperour begg'd for an end to the tryall, lest his daughter depart from this life. . . .

What Barth has finally created is, however, more than a pornographic joke; it is a counter-parable, an anti-stereotype of our beginnings in Virginia, in which Pocahontas' relationship to John Smith is portrayed not as an act of pure altruism and pity, but a sexual encounter so mechanical, so bestial, that it seems an assault rather than an act of love—and, therefore, a truer metaphor of our actual relations with the Indians than the pretty story so long celebrated in sentimental verse.

Barth does not leave his Indian Princess at the point of violation; he gives us a final glimpse of her after she has recovered her health and her desire: "As for the Princesse, she still lingers at the gate, all wystfullie, and sends him, by her attendants, woven basketts of great dry'd eggplants . . ." And it is basically so—as a whore begging to be screwed—that the anti-Pocahontas has flourished in the New Western ever since, growing fatter and fatter, as well as ever more slatternly and insatiable. In my own story, "The First Spade in the West," she appears as Fat Ellen, cadging drinks at a bar, cussing out the owner, "lurching and heavy footed even in too-large sneakers without laces"; and in David Markson's *The Ballad of Dingus Magee* (a hilarious burlesque on the growth of a gunslinger's reputation, rendered in straight-faced Faulknerian prose, and starring a certain "Captain Fiedler"), she enters as Hotwater Anna, "short and square-headed," stinking from her "thickly buttered hair," and crying, "You look for bim-bam, hey? Twenty-five cent, real hot damn bargain."

Perhaps the most elaborate recent portrait of such a type appears in the description of Indian Jenny which is woven in and out of the main action of Ken Kesey's second novel, *Sometimes a Great Notion:*

> . . . On this shield of cheekbone and forehead and chin are dabs of make-up that are arranged differently every day, though the expression beneath the make-up never changes. When her pension check arrives . . . she comes in to sit and celebrate the government's generosity by drinking one bourbon-over-snuff after another until . . . she rises to shuffle about the room in a heavy-footed dance, and always stumbles and always falls . . . across a table of fishermen or bushelers or truckdrivers . . . drunker than she . . . and then rises and takes a sleeve between stubby nail-painted fingers and squints into the face at the end of it: "You're drunk. You come on now. I'll take you home all right."

But the final degradation of Pocahontas into anti-Pocahontas, redeeming Princess into importunate prostitute, comes in James Leo Herlihy's *Midnight Cowboy,* in which we are given, as it were, a second-generation anti-Pocahontas, the offspring of an Indian whore grown old and rich enough to be a madame: but this time the blasphemed

Dusky Maiden is not even dark skinned, not quite a girl, but an almost albino faggot half-breed called Tombaby, though occasionally "Princess," too, by his mother:

> Tombaby Barefoot was a light-haired, pale, oddly constructed half-breed. He had a small head and no shoulders to speak of, but from his stomach to the ground he was big and thick and heavy. He wore a gray sweatshirt with HARVARD printed on it, faded and torn levis, sneakers, and a pair of gold earrings.

And the poor last Westerner of Herlihy's book, Joe Buck, is not merely pursued by Tombaby, but at last raped (after being knocked silly) in a nightmare parody of sex-in-the woods:

> ... Joe struggled to free himself and then a fist caught him in the stomach. ... On the edge of the bed he doubled over, trying to pull some air into him. ... Still he felt hands all over him and some of them were soft damp hands and they glided all over his back and along his thighs. Combining with the pain in his stomach these hands sickened him, and he began to retch and vomit. But nothing came out. Still the hands continued and one of them began to manipulate him in a surprising way that caused in him a kind of nightmare panic, and when he was able to achieve a little air, he used it to gird himself for further struggle. But at this point, a voice, Juanita's, said in a loud whisper, "You want it, Tombaby, they's only one way you gonna have it."

Not all unmaskings of the Indian Princess are so unrelievedly dark and queasy, however; even in Kesey's *Sometimes A Great Notion,* Jenny is presented sympathetically in the end, a kind of hidden High Priestess in her seedy crib on the beach—who searches vainly for her lapsed magical powers in Thomas Mann's *Magic Mountain,* the White man's Bible, Alastair Crawley, and Alan Watts, then finds them again in a game with oyster shells she had learned as a child. Evoking the face of an ideal beloved by manipulating them, she becomes once more her Indian self, a Sex-Goddess Pocahontas going to greet her alien lover, and lifting her skirts to reveal her sacred nakedness.

> Jenny steps back from the face before her, dropping her eyes.
> "Jenny . . . is that your name, Jenny?"
> "Yeah. Not really. People just allus call me Jenny."
> "And your real name?"
> "Leahnoomish. Means Brown Fern."
> "Lee-ah-noo-mish . . . Brown Fern. That is very pretty."
> "Yeah. Look here. You think I have pretty legs?"
> "Very pretty. And the skirt also. Very very pretty . . . little Brown Fern."
> "Haw," Jenny says triumphantly, lifting the mud-hemmed garment on off over her head.

The most successful rehabilitation of the archetypal Indian Maiden is to be found in Leonard Cohen's *Beautiful Losers*—a book of extraordinary elegance and grossness and truth—which simultaneously recounts the legend of Catherine Tekakwitha, the Mohawk girl who actually lived in seventeenth century Canada, and tells the contemporary tale of a polymorphous perverse triangle involving two men and a French Canadian young woman called Edith. As the novel progresses, the figure of Edith, utterly unfaithful to anything but her own passion, blurs into that of her Indian anti-type, who dedicated herself to a life of virginity for the sake of Christ—and died in the midst of fasting, prayer, and self-flagellation on the banks of the St. Lawrence; and the two become Isis, which is to say, the Great Goddess herself.

"I've come after you, Catherine Tekakwitha," Cohen's narrator begins. "I want to know what goes on under that rosy blanket. . . . I fell in love with a religious picture of you . . . God knows how far up your moccasins were laced . . . I have come to rescue you from the Jesuits." And he prays to his anti-Jesuitical God: "In the gloomy longhouse of my mind let me trade wives, let me stumble upon you, Catherine Tekakwitha, three hundred years old, fragrant as a birch sapling, no matter what the priests or plague have done to you."

At this point we begin to suspect that it is not *our* mythological girl that Cohen is redeeming, for all his insistence on the redness of her flesh: "Catherine Tekakwitha, I hope you are very dark. I want to detect a little whiff of raw meat and white blood on your thick black hair. I hope there is a little grease left in your thick black hair."

It is not from priest and plagues and the pledge of virginity that our Protestant Pocahontas must be rescued, but from the Courts of Kings and tobacco merchants and the threat of marriage. Just as our girl is a redskin Pamela, do what we will, Cohen's is a dusky Virgin, whatever he desires: "She lived in a woman's body but—it did not belong to her! It was not hers to offer! With a desperate slingshot thought she hurled her cunt forever into the night. . . . Ah, the pain eased, the torn flesh she finally did not own healed in its freedom, and a new description of herself, so brutally earned, forced itself into her heart: she was Virgin."

How different, finally, the WASP Pocahontas from the Roman Catholic one—or rather the WASP Pocahontases from the Roman Catholic ones, since there are two of each: for the WASPS, one in the early seventeenth century and one in the early nineteenth (Smith's Daughter of Powhatan, and Lewis and Clark's faithful "squar," Sacajawea); and for the R.C.'s, one from the cold north and one from the gentler south (the Jesuits' Catherine, and Cortez's Indian mistress, Marina). Yet in the end, in our time of a common Pop Culture, they blend together: the Planter's wife, the girl guide with a babe at her breast, the pure witness to the efficacy of faith, and the sultry mistress who provided a name for a late Shakespearean play; they bleach out under the impossibly bright lights of the movie set—become Marilyn Monroe.

The clue is there from the start in Cohen, when his narrator comments a page or two into his story, in the midst of his declaration of love for Catherine, "Lady Marilyn just died a few years ago. May I say that some old scholar four hundred years from now, maybe of my own blood, will come after her in the way I come after you?" And they have already begun to do so in fact, Cohen's own mentor, Irving Layton, for instance, in a brief elegiac poem, and Norman Mailer in the concluding pages of *An American Dream*.

It is inevitable, I suppose, that the Female Goddess, illegitimately dreamed by those whose religious commitments oblige them to reject her publicly, cease to be an Indian and turn into a marshmallow-white blonde when she becomes the fantasy, not of Anglo-Saxon palefaces and pallid, celibate priests, but of second-generation East European Jews. Precisely such counter-fantasies, however—of Jews, hippies, acid-heads—are the stuff of which the New Western is made, whether in novel form or on the screen. How apt, then, that the Pocahontas of Arthur Miller's first screenplay, *The Misfits* (in which no more than in his earlier work does he identify his characters or problems as Jewish, but in which at least he is past the hang-up of fighting out his oedipal conflicts and pretending they are the Class Struggle), be not only played by Marilyn Monroe, his then wife, but *be* Marilyn Monroe under whatever fictional name.

Miller, however, is a little baffling in this regard; for in that important (though failed) New Western, *The Misfits*, he seems also to be doing a travesty (perhaps unconsciously) of the *kitsch* parable at the center of *The Virginian* and *Riders of the Purple Sage* and *High Noon*. In Miller's version, however, the cards are stacked against the spokesman for the Code of the West, played by a dying Clark Gable; for this time the aging Westerner goes forth armed not with six-guns to destroy a villain, but only with a lasso to capture wild horses for the sake of making a buck. And confronting him is no schoolmarm or genteel

New England lady, for all her golden hair, but a Pagan Fertility Goddess—as we realize, if we have not already, in the scene where she embraces a tree with primordial passion authentic enough to belong to the archetypal red-brown nude of whom Pocahontas was the WASP's first avatar, but who had bleached out as early as the thirties to become Nathanael West's Faye Greener, possessed—in the dream of the Jew—by movie cowboy and Mexican, though lusted for in vain by artist and small-town square.

FROM GARY COOPER TO
LEE MARVIN

EVEN AS the mythological Indian heroine is altered (denigrated or sacramentalized, or both) in the New Western, so also is that WASP hero in the wilderness, her lover, descended from the equivocal figure of John Smith. We have noticed how Barth revealed the Captain himself as a boaster and trickster, whose very sexual prowess (the last vestige of manliness to which he can lay claim) comes from art rather than nature. And his latter-day offspring tend to become ever more diminished. Sometimes they decay from within, ending up as only their outsides, an emptiness in chaps and sombrero like the Earle Shoop of *Day of the Locust*, or the male hustler in Western garb of Herlihy's *Midnight Cowboy* with his dream of making all the rich women in New York, or the Guard of Honor around a corpse at the end of my own story, "The First Spade in the West," each member of which wears the conventional costume like a disguise:

> Meanwhile, there they were in full cowboy outfits, all four of them, because that was the way Elmira had wanted it: chaps and bandanas, high heel boots and spurs, and a ten-gallon hat on the chair behind each of them, the works. . . . At the last minute, Wally had said they should wear six-guns, too . . . but Tommie hadn't seen it like that at all, so they had split the difference and settled for empty holsters . . . a beatnik from the East, a little sheeny with a shoe-clerk's mus-

tache, a big fat queer who'd struck it rich, and a spade. . . .

Sometimes, though they remain more solid, the new Western anti-heroes shrink in size until they move through the vastness of the West more like the dwarfed Julius Rodman of Edgar Allan Poe than any movie version of the Cowboy Hero—except some of those projected by Alan Ladd (say, Shane), who, to make mythological amends for his physiological lack of size, was always given the benefit of an invisible box to stand on. Certainly, Dingus Magee is not only small but scrawny; and Thomas Berger's Little Big Man is precisely what his name declares: a shrimp with sharp wits and an enormous spirit—though in a showdown he prefers to depend more on those wits than that spirit, as, for instance, in encounters with the sort of large, icy killer he knows he cannot outdraw, best exemplified in Berger's book by Wild Bill Hickok. Finally, Wild Bill fares worse than Berger's invented protagonist; indeed, all of the "historical" characters in *Little Big Man* are undercut and debunked by a kind of merciless geniality that is likely to mislead the unwary reader about the real nature of the novel.

One reviewer, for example, quite inappropriately described *Little Big Man,* just after it had appeared, as "exciting, violent, and ribald . . . ranks with *The Big Sky* and *The Oxbow Incident.*" But it has neither the moral earnestness of the latter nor the easy realism of the former, only a desire to demonstrate how, for all its pathos and danger, the West was and remains essentially *funny:* Custer making his last stand (the Indians, we learn, refused to scalp him not out of respect, but because that vain and long-haired bully was growing bald); Wild Bill drawing his fatal poker hand; or any of the varied rest playing themselves so earnestly, Wyatt Earp, Calamity Jane, York the Slave. Once the debunking has begun, there is no end; everything is turned into the kind of joke on history that we play in return for the joke history has played on us: the Graduate Student's

Revenge. Berger is not so brutal and extreme in this regard, so totally nihilistic as David Markson, or even John Barth; but he, too, cannot resist drawing almost anything he happens to know into the circle of his ridicule, reporting, for instance, of Jack Crabb's six-foot-high ugly sister:

> In time she fell in love with a man she met in a military hospital near Washington, D. C. . . . He was not a casualty but rather a male nurse . . . a real cultivated person who went so far as to write poetry in his spare time. . . . According to Caroline, he was shy but she felt sure he returned her feeling, for he gave her some of his writings and it was full of burning passion. . . . I see no need to go through the whole story, for the point is that when this fellow got to where he saw Caroline was in great sympathy with him, he confessed he was in love with a curly-headed little drummer boy. . . . I remember this individual's name, but I ain't going to mention it, for he got quite a reputation in later times for his robustious verse. . . .

One thing only escapes dissolution in the compulsive anti-mythical burlesque of such books—the hero's ability to satisfy sexually all women, including and especially Indian ones; and the ante is progressively raised from the one Pocahontas whom, according to *The Sot-Weed Factor*, Smith so astonishingly serviced. Jack Crabb, for instance, takes on three of various ages and sizes in a single night (while his Indian wife is giving birth outside the teepee), and Dingus does much better. "Dean Goose," Anna Hotwater asks at one point, "feller stop one time up to Injun camp near Fronteras? Feller take on seventeen squaws in twenty hours nonstop and squish the belly-button out'n every damn one?" Only they never stay with any of the women they make love to or temporarily take as wives, any of these potent but perambulating New Westerners; nor do the children their women bear them survive to become New Men in a New World. Quite like Huck Finn, or the Cowboys in the Saturday afternoon movies of our childhood, they always light out for the Territory ahead of a total commitment.

Implicit in the Pocahontas legend from the very beginning, since it is essentially a myth of Indian assimilation to WASP-dom (more pretentiously, Europe or Christianity), is the Happy Ending of marriage and the begetting of children to inherit the wealth—tobacco, in the first instance—of the Indians' America. But even John Smith leaves that conclusion to his strange *alter ego,* John Rolfe, whom the genealogical tables of Virginia remember, but the mythological memory of Americans forgets. That New Race, of which Lawrence dreamed, cannot be begotten of a union in the body, but only of a spiritual marriage; and that marriage, the earliest texts tell us and our classic literature endlessly repeats, is of male to male, Alexander Henry to Wawatam, Natty Bumppo to Chingachgook, Gordon Pym to Dirk Peters, etc., etc., the archetypal equivalent of WASP assimilation to the world of the Indian. In this myth, too, tobacco plays a part, not as a commodity, however, but as "medicine," magic, a means of communion. Men whom the bottle sunders (that source of bad "medicine," which infuriates the Indian not only to kill, but even to commit the White man's assault of rape), the pipe joins together.

Each time Jack Crabb, for instance, returns to the tent of Old Lodge Skins, who is his friend, brother, father, grandfather (it is the last title which he prefers), to whom alone he is faithful, among all his loves, until death separates them, they smoke " 'We must smoke your return,' he said, and went through the rigamarole of filling the pipe, lighting it, offering it to the four points of the compass and so on . . ." Crabb reports of their first reunion, and of their last, "Finally I says: 'Grandfather I did not expect to see you.' 'Nor I you, my son,' answers Old Lodge Skins. 'Do you want to smoke?' " And out of their communion, Jack Crabb is reborn each time as his own child and the Indian's, a man neither white nor Indian because he is both, and therefore capable of a kind of cosmic vision denied him by his European heritage: "I wasn't wobbling no more. I was there, in movement, yet at the center of the world, where all is self-explanatory merely because it *is*. . . ."

Crabb cannot hold on to his vision, nor his author to a hope for its survival: "I am a white man and never forgot it . . ." the first sentence of Crabb's chronicle begins; and what else is there for him to be in a world from which the Indian is felt to be vanishing, in which even Old Lodge Skins foresees that his own people and their kind of life "must eventually pass from the face of the earth"? Strange how in one of the very books in which the Vanishing American returns, its author doubts the reality of that reappearance; to be sure, the old Indian who is his spokesman says before his death that the Cheyenne at least "will live on in whatever men are fierce and strong. So that when women see a man who is proud and brave and vengeful, even if he has a white face, they will cry, 'That is a Human Being!' " But that is far from Lawrence's prophecy of a new race—a woman's view, or worse, a man's fantasy of a woman's view, as the text itself confesses.

And, anyhow, Thomas Berger will not quite let us believe any of it, undercutting all of his assertions with the ironies implicit in his narrative frame. The story is told to us by a neurotic queer just recovering from a bad breakdown, and purports to be his recollection of a story told *him* by a self-styled 111-year-old in the psychiatric ward of a State Hospital. "I have never been able to decide on how much of Mr. Crabb's story to believe . . ." the frame-narrator confesses toward the close. "Jack Crabb was either the most neglected hero in the history of this country or a liar of insane proportions." What has shaken him is the fact that he has checked the records and found no evidence to confirm even Crabb's existence, much less his adventures: "But one name is missing from every index, every roster, every dossier. . . ."

Precisely here, of course, is the problem (and the consequent opportunity for irony) for everyone who tries to evoke in fiction the meaning of the West by reconstructing its past. Two kinds of truth come immediately into conflict, and the writer is tempted to choose: the truth of history, which is the truth of reason; and the truth of myth, which is the truth of madness. It is possible to have it both ways, of course, for the fictionist as opposed to the historian; Leonard Cohen, for instance, shifts from an original narrator who is scholar, deeply immersed in the *Jesuit Relations*, to an institutionalized madman, who is lost in his own dreams, in order to recover for us the image of the seventeenth century Indian saint and her relevance to our lives now.

There is a question of sympathy involved, too; and finally our writers divide in their allegiance: some, like Cohen (and Ken Kesey) betraying a lust for un-reason, a nostalgia for a time when insanity could be heroically lived out in a landscape indistinguishable from nightmare; some, like Thomas Berger (and David Markson) revealing a final commitment to rationality, a preference for the kind of order scholarship can impose on what has merely happened —and for the kind of jokes one can make at the expense of myth, once he has perceived that order.

I am not meaning to say that there is not madness everywhere in Berger's book as well as Cohen's; after all, Crabb's sister ends up in the nuthouse in the course of his yarn, and he himself follows her there, after its close, despite the final prayer of his Indian "grandfather": "Take care of my son here . . . and see that he does not go crazy!" Nonetheless, the prayer does work for Berger, at least, for the author if not the character. And having chosen sanity, he has in effect settled for satire; just as, choosing madness, other writers commit themselves to sentimentality. Obviously, sentimentality and satire can be and are intermingled in varying proportions, in the New Western as in other literary forms; but once more it is a question of final allegiance.

Without a commitment to sentimentality, the New Western remains—though often amusing, and sometimes even terrifying as well—more a comment on traditional notions of the making of Americans than a radical reconstruction of such notions. The "New Race" which Lawrence foresaw (and toward which, with or without benefit of literature, we are evolving at an astonishing rate) demands a New Myth. When it depends chiefly on satire, however, the New Western converts the stereotypes of the *kitsch* Western not into myth, or even anti-myth, but only into anti-stereotype: Pop Art on its lowest level. Anti-John Smiths and anti-Pocahontases are neither fictional embodiments nor dream-projections of our presently developing life-style, but only cartoon versions of what we find unviable in our legendary past.

Nor does the super-Pocahontas, Pocahontas as Native Earth Goddess, satisfy our deepest mythical longings, Hart Crane to the contrary nothwithstanding. Even Cohen's *Beautiful Losers*, for all its elegant grossness, does not fill the bill; perhaps because its Jewish revision of a Roman Catholic archetype remains as alien to our own mythological West as the original version of Tekakwitha was to that of Pocahontas. In Cohen's novel, the Indian Maiden loses her specific American meanings and fades into a more general European-Near Eastern archetype of female sexuality—thus dissolving *our* West once more into the larger Occident. And the men who survive Catherine in *Beautiful Losers*—after seeming for a little while to possess her and each other in and through her—are sundered even from each other (as irrevocably as scholarship is sundered from psychosis) to dream not the New Race of D. H. Lawrence, but what Cohen calls the "New Jew." But these are, in the world of myth, polar opposites.

How could they be otherwise, since Lawrence's fundamental anti-Semitism was never more operative in his thinking than when he reflected on the fate of America? This is somewhat more obvious in the earlier versions of the essays which make up *Studies in Classic American Literature* than in the finally revised form, though it is present by implication there, too. Comparing the two possibilities which lie before Americans, Lawrence wrote originally:

> We have a latent craving to control from our deliberate will the very springing and welling-up of the life-impulse itself. This craving, once admitted becomes a lust. . . . The Jews of old became established in this lust: hence their endless purifications . . . hence also the rite of circumcision, the setting of the seal of self-conscious will upon the very quick of bodily impulse. . . . The great field for the lust of control in the modern world is America. . . . The perfection of machine triumph, of deliberate self-determined motion, is to be found in the Americans and the Jews. . . . Only Americans and Jews suffer from a torturing frictional unease, an incapacity to rest. . . .
>
> And yet it cannot be for this alone that millions have crossed the Ocean. . . . This is not the reality of America. . . . There will come an America we cannot foretell, a new creation on the face of the earth . . . the mechanical monstrosity of the west will presently disappear.

How different from this primordial fear of circumcision, this horror-vision of Election and Law as castration, is Cohen's counter-dream of a saving remnant eternally chosen and marked off from others by circumcision at least of the heart:

> Who is the New Jew?
> The New Jew loses his mind gracefully. . . . He has induced amnesia by a repetitious study of history, his very forgetfulness caressed by facts which he accepts with visible enthusiasm. He changes for a thousand years the value of stigma, causing men of all nations

to pursue it as superior sexual talisman. . . . He uses regret as a bulwark of originality. . . . He confirms tradition through amnesia, tempting the whole world with rebirth. He dissolves history and ritual by accepting unconditionally the complete heritage. . . . Sometimes he is Jewish but always he is American. . . .

And yet the anti-Semitic, anti-puritanical Puritan from England strikes closer to the mythological truth for which our own anti-puritanical Puritan hearts yearn, even when we are Jews more or less at home in America. For he knew something else, too, which we are born not knowing we know, being born on this soil—something which demanded a stranger, a sojourner, to point it out for the first time: that the essential myth of the West and, therefore, of ourselves, is not the myth of John Smith and Pocahontas, no matter how we invert or distort it, but the myth of Natty Bumppo and Chingachgook. Here is, for us—for better or for worse, and apparently forever—the heart of the matter: the confrontation in the wilderness of the White European refugee from civilization and the "stern, imperturbable warrior." Apparently, Lawrence did not know the story of Alexander Henry and Wawatam which precedes even Cooper's version; but what Cooper dreamed, he knew and understood, perceiving that this union rather than that into which Pocahontas's adventure with Smith inducted her, the marriage with John Rolfe, was the fruitful one: that from the nonconsummated marriage of males the New Race would come.

That which Chingachgook was, Natty was not; nor could he ever know. In the same way, Natty himself was the untranslatable unknown to Chingachgook. Yet across this unsuperable gulf in being there passed some strange communion . . . a quality of pure unknowable embrace. And out of this embrace arises the strange wing-covered seraph of a new race-being. . . .

In the very tone and rhetoric of the passage, the peculiar brand of sentimentality is revealed which underlies all genuinely mythic descriptions of the West, all true Westerns—a kind of Higher Masculine Sentimentality utterly remote from all fables whose Happy Ending is Marriage.

THE HIGHER SENTIMENTALITY

PRIMITIVISM IS THE large generic name for the Higher Masculine Sentimentality, a passionate commitment to inverting Christian-Humanist values, out of a conviction that the Indian's way of life is preferable. From this follows the belief that if one is an Indian he ought, despite missionaries and school boards, to remain Indian; and if one is White, he should do his best, despite all pressures of the historical past, to go Native. Ever since the oft-quoted observation of Crèvecoeur that there must be something superior in Indian society since "thousands of Europeans are Indians, and we have no example of even one of those aborigines having from choice become Europeans . . . ," White men in America have continued to echo that primitivist hyperbole, whose truth cannot be diminished merely by disproving Crèvecoeur's facts.

Crèvecoeur's own *Letters from an American Farmer* ends with a declaration that he is about to pack up his family and head out for a wigwam in the forest, a resolution which, once he had written it down, he felt quite free not to live. But this seems irrelevant; for, in theory at least, the rejection of Our Side and the identification with Theirs involved in purely literary renegadism ought to be as disturbingly real as the act, say, of Simon Girty going over to the redskin enemy.

Yet, in fact, most of the literature written by literary renegades affords us only the easy pleasure and secondhand self-righteousness once derived by Victorians from reading about the tribulations of the poor. Even a symbolic desertion to the Indians should seem an outrage, a blasphemy—certainly not just another pious gesture, one more Good Work. But precisely this sense of do-gooding mars for me the would-be primitivism of certain authors who, in addition to loving Indians and propagandizing on their behalf, lived with them and knew them intimately: Oliver La Farge, for instance, whose *Laughing Boy* was once taken very seriously indeed, and Frank Waters, whose *The Man Who Killed the Deer* is once again in print twenty-five years after its first appearance.

The pretense of writing from within the consciousness of Indians intrinsic to such fiction leaves me always with the sense of having confronted an act of impersonation rather than one of identification, a suspicion of having been deceived; and this is reinforced when the presumable wisdom of the alien Red Man turns out to be some quite familiar cliché of our own culture—as when toward the end of Waters' novel, Byers, his surrogate and spokesman, thinks:

> We are all caught in the tide of perpetual change. These pueblos, these reservations must sometime pass away, and the red flow out into the engulfing white. . . . So both must sometime pass: the Indian with his simple fundamental premise untranslated into modern terms, and finally the white with his monstrous materiality.
>
> But perhaps there would still be time, thought Byers, to learn from these people before they pass from this earth which was theirs and is now all men's—the simple and monstrous truth of mankind's solidarity with all that breathes and does not breathe . . .

The book ends not on this relatively somber note, however, but with a temporary Happy Ending, the postponement of the Vanishing American's vanishing for one more generation, as the Sacred Lake is saved for the tribe, and yet one more boy adopted into a kiva to be initiated into the old ways.

Despite such concessions to Hollywood taste, however, Waters' book has a continuing appeal to the young, whose disaffection from a life dedicated to work and success makes them susceptible to even the *kitsch*iest evocations of the Indian alternatives. It would be hard to understand otherwise how such a conventional example of slick fiction as William Eastlake's "Portrait of an Artist With 26 Horses" (about an Indian who gives up living in the white man's world, believing this involves giving up his wife and son, only to discover that they are waiting for him, having learned on their own such bits of esoteric wisdom as "money isn't everything" and "it won't buy happiness") was included in a recent collection made by Donald Allen and Robert Creeley, calling itself *New American Story*.

A more considerable and impressive try at the same sort of thing is Peter Matthiessen's *At Play in the Fields of the Lord*, which recounts at its center the story of a college-educated, brainwashed North American Indian called Lewis Meriwether Moon by a romantic father who had loved the memory of that doomed explorer for having crossed the continent without—he had been convinced—killing a single Indian. Moon, a mercenary soldier with a patched-up plane as his stock-in-trade and a Jewish hipster for a partner, finds himself among still primitive South American tribesmen; appalled at the emptiness of his own life, the lovelessness of his own world, he makes it back to nakedness and mindlessness in the jungle mud.

There is much in Matthiessen's book that is palpably false (his hippy Jew from the Bronx is incredible, his white missionaries stereotypes out of Somerset Maugham); but he renders with real convincingness the downward progress of Moon: first detaching himself by will from one way of life, then falling by necessity out of another, until, in utter loneliness, he recapitulates the beginning or invents the end of man. And at that extreme moment, he mourns the passing of his people, even before he bewails himself:

. . . a well of sadness for things irredeemable and gone flowed over him. The Indian nation had grown old; he knelt down like a penitent and wept. He wept for Aeore and the doomed people of the jungle, and he wept for the last old leatherfaces of the plains. . . .

He felt bereft, though of what he did not know. He was neither white nor Indian, man nor animal. . . .

He thought, Am I the first man on the earth; am I the last?

Finally, such works depend upon a pathos too simple, a world-view too naive, to sustain a major literary effort, however adequate they may seem to the living needs of the young. I, at any rate, have never been as much moved by any of the fictions derived from nostalgic primitivism as by a letter written me just after the death of Hemingway and my own published responses to it. Composed by a young Montanan who had just attended a meeting of the Native American Church, an Indian peyote cult with fundamentalist Christian trimmings, it is a deliberate non-literary, even anti-literary document; and maybe this is part of the real point, since a novel in praise of the analphabetic past stirs more ironies than it can ever resolve. "I hope you will pardon this midsummer madness," the letter begins, and "madness" is the keynote, my correspondent continuing a little later:

> Since attending an all night prayer meeting with . . . the Cheyenne I am also mad on Indians. I expected to have hallucinations, I did not expect to encounter truths. . . . What one sees, and this has no meaning (I suppose) until one has seen it, is one's mirror image, the image everyone (especially Hemingway) is secretly searching for, the answer to the question "What am I *really* like?" . . .

If Hemingway obsesses the writer, it is because Hemingway seems to him what he in fact was—except in the facetious talking-in-his-sleep of *Torrents of Spring*—the inventor for our time of the False Western. Hemingway (along with books and the movies) lies; the Indians (along with drum-beating and peyote) tell the truth: this is the simple-minded thesis.

> The mental mirror of the conqueror cannot be found in the culture of the conqueror. The mental mirror of the conqueror can only be found in the eyes of the conquered, those people who do not read or write or leave histories or legends, but simply live and die unremembered. It took hours of fire watching and drum-beating and chanting and meditation before that deepest of liberal prejudices, that underneath the skin we are all alike, finally wore off. . . . We are bred and inculcated from childhood in the doctrines and belief of winners. We are conquerors, upmen, all of us, collectively and individually. (The Jews, being a traditionally conquered people, get off more easily, but only in a relative way.)

Perhaps the parenthetical comment suggests one reason why Jews have played so large a role in creating the New or anti-"Upman" Western Novel; though, as a matter of fact, they did not begin to do so until, in America and especially in the field of the arts, they began to move rapidly into the establishment, i.e., to go "up."

> I cannot think of a single Hemingway hero, who was not, in one way or another, a conqueror's hero. Brave, stoic, modest, essentially unanalytic, never grasping, dedicated to honor in the face of events which made honor meaningless. . . . We conquerors heroize Gary Cooper and Natty Bumppo, because by pretending that they are really like us, we are able to create a mirror image of ourselves that is pleasing. . . .
> The mirror image that the American public has loved to find for itself in the Hemingway novels is the opposite of the true mirror image of the American public. Those of us who have come close to the pio-

neers in Montana know . . . those great heroes of the west, eulogized Monday through Friday on TV, were the most selfish, ruthless, cunning, conniving, grasping bastards in the history of the World. And to cover this up . . . they imitated, mimicked, mocked and claimed for themselves the nature of the person they tortured and murdered, the American Indian. No wonder the only good Indian is a dead Indian. They give the lie to the frontier myth. . . . The frontier heroes were mock Indians. . . .

At this point, my correspondent might well have sat down to write just such a satire of the Old West as David Markson produced in *The Ballad of Dingus Magee*. But, remembering Hemingway, he turns in another direction:

Anyway, the thesis which I never got to is that Hemingway is the colossal literary upman, playing the winner's game all the way. Like all good Nazis (racial upmen) he went nuts at the end. The Indians are colossal downmen (they are too lazy to write). While we have been playing checkers they have been playing give away. As a result they have nothing but poverty, anonymity, happiness, lack of neuroses, wonderful children and a way of life that is free, democratic and in complete fulfillment of the American dream, the one Hemingway longed for.

And as a final note, an obvious afterthought, he adds (thus emboldening me to use his text as I have):

I personally have joined the Cheyenne and am never going to use this thesis. I'm playing give away.

Madness, drugs, caricature, and abuse: many of the essentials of the New Western are already present here; but the setting will not do, for finally the Reservation (half island in time, half ghetto in space) is as inadequate a West in the latter half of the twentieth century as the remembered forests of Barth and Cohen, or the remote ones of Matthiessen. La Farge and Waters and Eastlake and even my friend fresh from firewatching in Montana are seeking the West in a past which is not less lapsed because it has been preserved in a few enclaves, flanked by motels and souvenir shops, and connected by superhighways. If there still exists for us a Wilderness and a Place-out-of-Time appropriate for renewal rather than nostalgia, rebirth rather than recreation, that place must be in the Future, not the Past: that Future toward which we have been pointed ever since the Super-Guy comic books and the novels of science fiction shifted the orientation of Pop Art by one hundred and eighty degrees.

But the real opposite of nostalgic is psychedelic, the reverse of remembering is hallucinating, which means that, insofar as the New Western is truly New, it, too, must be psychedelic.

The term is embarrassingly fashionable and disconcertingly broad in application, including, in the field of fiction alone, examples as varied as science fiction itself, both in its classic form, and in such extensions as Burrough's *Nova Express*, Harry Matthew's *Tlooth*, and Anthony Burgess' *The Clockwork Orange;* metapolitical fables, emerging out of the wreck of Marxist ideology, like the story behind that astonishing movie, *Morgan;* and even such High Church Christian allegories, pretending to be fairy tales, as J. R. R. Tolkien's *The Lord of the Rings*. But no other name fits as well the New Western, which, like the Old Western at its most authentic, deals precisely with the alteration of consciousness.

Besides, many of the so-called "psychedelics" themselves, those hallucinogenic drugs, at least, found in nature rather than synthesized in the laboratory (marijuana, peyote, the Mexican Mushroom, Ayahuasca, etc.), are our bridge to—even as they are gifts from—the world of the Indian: the world not of an historical past, but of the eternally archaic one. And so, too, are those other once-magical plants, now long socialized and deprived of power, *yerba maté,* coffee, cacao, and, especially, tobacco, on which Shamans once saw visions—and which somehow still threatens us Whites, as our Big Medicine, whiskey ("The White Man's Milk," the Indians called it), still threatens the Indian. It is easy to forget how those first hippies of the Western World, Raleigh, Marlowe, and company, cultivated a life-style based on homosexuality, a contempt for Established Religion, and "drinking" tobacco; for all that survives of the first Indian-inspired Drug Cult are a handful of lyrics, apt to strike us as much more amusing than dangerous:

> The Indian weed withered quite,
> Green at morn, cut down at night,
> Shows thy decay;
> All flesh is hay:
> Thus think, then drink Tobacco.

Nothing in the seventeenth century compares in scope and avowed seriousness even with the literature of the nineteenth century Drug Cult (centered around opiates, and therefore implicated in the myth of an Absolute East rather than a Polar West), from Poe and Coleridge and DeQuincy to Baudelaire—much less with the prose and verse being composed now on, or in the name of, "pot." Certainly it is hard to identify a tobacco-style, as one can an opium-style, and even a marijuana (or, as we come to synthesize a Super-West of our own, an LSD) one.

In Cohen's *Beautiful Losers,* for instance, the sort of vision evoked by psychedelics, or bred by the madness toward which their users aspire, is rendered in a kind of prose appropriate to that vision—a prose hallucinated and even, it seems to me, hallucinogenic: a style by which it is possible to be actually turned on, though only perhaps (judging by the critical resistance to Cohen's book) if one is already tuned in to the times. Yet even he felt a need for an allegiance to the past as well as the future, to memory as well as madness—or perhaps more accurately a need to transmute memory into madness, dead legend into living hallucination; and for him the myth of Catherine Tekakwitha served that purpose.

For us, however, on the other side of a border that is religious as well as political, mythological as well as historical, her story will not work; and what we demand in its place is the archetypal account of no analogous girl (for us women make satisfactory devils, but inadequate saints), but the old, old fable of the White outcast and the noble Red Man joined together against home and mother, against the female world of civilization. This time, however, we require a new setting, at once present and archaic—a setting which Ken Kesey discovered in the madhouse: *our* kind of madhouse, which is to say, one located in the American West, so that the Indian can make his reappearance in its midst with some probability, as well as real authenticity.

Perhaps it was necessary for Kesey to come himself out of Oregon, one of our last actual Wests (just as it was necessary for him to have been involved with one of the first experiments with the controlled use of LSD), since for most Americans after Mark Twain, the legendary colored companion of the white fugitive had been turned from Red to Black. Even on the most naive levels, the Negro has replaced the Indian as the natural enemy of Woman; as in the recent film *The Fortune Cookie,* for instance, the last scene of which fades out on a paleface *schlemiel* (delivered at last from his treacherous whore of a white wife) tossing a football back and forth with his Negro buddy in a deserted football stadium. Similarly, in such sophisticated fiction as James Purdy's *Cabot Wright Begins,* the color scheme demanded by the exigencies of current events is observed, though in this case, the relationship has become overtly and explicitly homosexual:

> . . . His dark-skinned prey seated himself under the street-lamp and Bernie, more desperate by the moment, seated himself next to him, then almost immediately introduced himself.

His new friend accepted the introduction in the manner in which it was meant. They exchanged the necessary information about themselves, Bernie learning that his chance acquaintance was Winters Hart, from a town in the Congo. . . . Taking Winters Hart's left hand in his, Bernie held his friend's dark finger on which he wore a wedding-ring, and pressed the finger and the hand.

Far from being annoyed at this liberty, Winters Hart was, to tell the truth, relieved and pleased. Isolation in a racial democracy, as he was to tell Bernie later that night, as they lay in Bernie's bed together, isolation, no thank you.

The title of the chapter from Purdy's book from which this passage comes is "One Flew East, One Flew West"—referring, I suppose, to the two sexual choices open to men; but it reminds us of the title of Kesey's archetypal Western, *One Flew Over the Cuckoo's Nest*, which represents a third possibility of White transcendence: madness itself.

A myth in which the non-White partner for whom the European American yearns is Black rather than Red, we tend to interpret as a parable of an attempt to extend our sexuality, to recover our lost *libido;* while one in which the White man longs for an Indian, we are likely to read as signifying a desire to breach the limits of reason, to extend our consciousness. Mark Twain tried valiantly to reverse this in his two books involving Huck Finn, making Injun Joe rather than Nigger Jim the threat to white womanhood; but trying in *Pudd'nhead Wilson* to imagine the only really sexually desirable woman in all his works, he felt obliged to make her minimally and by legal definition Black. Moreover, future Jims all the way down to Purdy's Winters Hart have tended to become ever more frankly the objects of *eros*. And this is fair enough, since in the language of archetype the Negro stands for alien passion, and the Indian for alien perception. (Or perhaps this is only another way of saying that at the level of deep imagination the Indian is male and the Negro female; the former Yang, the latter Yin.)

In no case does the longing for a Negro companion represent in the male a temptation to escape society once and for all by the final expedient of going out of one's head. Ike McCaslin in Faulkner's "The Bear," seems at first glance an exception; but the Sam Fathers who initiates him into lifelong isolation remains quite ambiguous, being Negro and Indian at the same time, maybe more Indian than Negro in the heart of the wilderness, where the crisis of the tale is enacted. In Faulkner's later work, his boy-heroes are humanized by their Negro mentors, saved for society rather than persuaded to abandon it by those bland, resilient post-Uncle Toms like Lucas Beauchamp. To be sure, an occasional female in Faulkner may have her madness compounded by the Negro upon whom she projects it, like Joanna Burden in *Light in August*, infuriated rather than satiated by the sexuality of Joe Christmas, who may, indeed, be less a Negro than a pretender to Negro-ness.

Even the most nearly lunatic of Faulkner's projections of his youthful self, Quentin Compson, is pushed over the brink not by finding a Negro Companion, but by failing to find one. His suicide on the verge of manhood may have been precipitated in part by a lifelong obsession with the impurity of White women, symbolized for him by his sister Caddy's soiled underpants; but it is more immediately occasioned by the absence in Cambridge of anything closer to a true Uncle Tom than Deacon, who blasphemously camps the role. Finally, Faulkner can imagine no America without the Negro—and when he tries to imagine someone like himself imagining it, he conceives of him wigging out of that world completely. But his Indians (the old Ikemotubbe, for instance, of his short stories) are vanishing by definition, disappearing as fast as the forests of the American past.

Not so with Ken Kesey, whose novel opens with an obviously psychotic "I" reflecting on his guards, one of whom identifies him almost immediately, speaking in a Negro voice: "Here's the Chief. The *soo*-pah Chief, fellas. Ol' Chief Broom. Here you go, Chief Broom. . . ." Chief Bromden is his real name, this immense schizophrenic, pretending he is deaf-and-dumb to baffle "the Combine," which he believes controls the world: "Look at him: a giant janitor. There's your Vanishing American, a six-foot-six sweeping machine, scared of its own shadow. . . ." Or rather Bromden is the name he has inherited from his white mother, who subdued the full-blooded Chief who sired him and was called "The-Pine-That-Stands-Tallest-on-the-Moutain." "He fought it a long time," the half-breed son comments at one point, "till my mother made him too little to fight any more and he gave up."

Chief Bromden believes he is little, too, what was left in him of fight and stature subdued by a second mother, who presides over the ward in which he is confined ("She may be a mother, but she's big as a damn barn and tough as knife metal . . .") and, at one point, had given him two hundred successive shock treatments. Not only is Mother II big, however, especially in the breasts; she is even more essentially *white:* "Her face is smooth, calculated, and precision-made, like an expensive baby doll, skin like flesh-colored enamel, blend of white and cream and baby-blue eyes . . ." and her opulent body is bound tight in a starched white uniform. To understand her in her full mythological significance, we must recall that seventeenth century first White Mother of Us All, Hannah Duston, and her struggle against the Indians who tried to master her.

Hannah has represented from the start those forces in the American community—soon identified chiefly with the female and maternal—which resist all incursions of savagery, no matter what their course. But only in the full twentieth century is the nature of Hannah's assault made quite clear, first in Freudian terms and then in psychedelic ones. "No, buddy," Kesey's white hero, Randle Patrick McMurphy, comments on the Big Nurse. "She ain't pecking at your *eyes*. That's not what she's peckin' at." And when someone, who really knows but wants to hear spoken aloud what he is too castrated to say, asks at *what*, then, R. P. McMurphy answers, "At your balls, buddy, at your everlovin' *balls*." Yet toward the close of the book, McMurphy has to be told by the very man who questioned him earlier the meaning of his own impending lobotomy at the hands of Big Nurse ("Yes, chopping away the brain. Frontal-lobe castration. I guess if she can't cut below the belt she'll do it above the eyes"), though by this time he understands why he, as well as the Indian (only victim of the original Hannah's blade), has become the enemy of the White Woman.

In his own view, McMurphy may be a swinger, and in the eyes of his Indian buddy an ultimate Westerner, the New American Man: "He walked with long steps, too long, and he had his thumbs hooked in his pockets again. The iron in his boot heels cracked lightning out of the tile. He was the logger again, the swaggering gambler . . . the cowboy out of the TV set walking down the middle of the street to meet a dare."

But to Big Nurse—and the whole staff of the asylum whom, White or Black, male or female, she has cowed—he is only a "psychopath," not less sick for having chosen the nuthouse in which he finds himself to the work-farm to which his society had sentenced him. And she sees the purpose of the asylum as being precisely to persuade men like him to accept and function in the world of rewards and punishments which he has rejected and fled.

To do this, however, she must persuade him like the rest that he is only a "bad boy," *her* bad boy, quite like, say Huckleberry Finn. But where Huck's substitute mothers demanded that he give up smoking, wear shoes, go to school, she asks (it is the last desperate version of "sivilisation") that he be sane: "All he has to do is *admit* he was wrong, to indicate, *demonstrate* rational contact and the treatment would be cancelled this time."

The choice is simple: either sanity abjectly accepted, or

sanity imposed by tranquilizers, shock treatments, finally lobotomy itself. But McMurphy chooses instead if not madness, at least aggravated psychopathy and an alliance with his half-erased, totally schizophrenic Indian comrade—an alliance with all that his world calls unreason, quite like that which bound Henry to Wawatam, Natty Bumppo to Chingachgook, even Ishmael to Queequeg (that versatile Polynesian, who, at the moment of betrothal, whips out a tomahawk pipe, quite as if he were a real Red Man). And this time, the alliance is not merely explicitly, but quite overtly directed against the White Woman, which is to say, Hannah Duston fallen out of her own legend into that of Henry and Wawatam.

For a while, the result seems utter disaster, since McMurphy, driven to attempt the rape of his tormentor, is hauled off her and duly lobotomized, left little more than a vegetable with "a face milk-white except for the heavy purple bruises around the eyes." Whiter than the White Woman who undid him, white as mother's milk: this is McMurphy at the end, except that Chief Bromden will not let it be the end, will not let "something like that sit there in the day room with his name tacked on it for twenty or thirty years so the Big Nurse could use it as an example of what can happen if you buck the system. . . ."

Therefore in the hush of the first night after the lobotomy, he creeps into the bed of his friend for what turns out to be an embrace—for only in a caricature of the act of love can he manage to kill him: "The big, hard body had a tough grip on life. . . . I finally had to lie full length on top of it and scissor the kicking legs with mine. . . . I lay there on top of the body for what seemed like days. . . . Until it was still a while and had shuddered once and was still again."

It is the first real *Liebestod* in our long literature of love between white men and colored, and the first time, surely, that the Indian partner in such a pair has outlived his White brother. Typically, Chingachgook had predeceased Natty, and Queequeg, Ishmael; typically, Huck had been younger than Jim, Ike than Sam Fathers. Everyone who has lived at the heart of our dearest myth knows that it is the white boy-man who survives, as the old Indian, addressing the Great Spirit, prepares to vanish. Even so recent a novel as Berger's *Little Big Man* has continued to play it straight, closing on the traditional dying fall, as Old Lodge Skins subsides after a final prayer, and his white foster son says:

> He laid down then on the damp rocks and died right away. I descended to the treeline, fetched back some poles, and built him a scaffold. Wrapped him in the red blanket and laid him thereon. Then after a while I started down the mountain in the fading light.

But on the last page of *One Flew Over the Cuckoo's Nest,* Chief Bromden is on his way back to the remnants of his tribe who "have took to building their old ramshackle wood scaffolding all over the big million-dollar . . . spillway." And his very last words are: "I been away a long time."

It is, then, the "Indian" in Kesey himself, the undischarged refugee from a madhouse, the AWOL Savage, who is left to boast: *And I only am escaped alone to tell thee.* But the "Indian" does not write books; and insofar as Kesey's fable can be read as telling the truth about himself as well as about all of us, it prophesies silence for him, a silence into which he has, in fact, lapsed, though not until he had tried one more Gutenberg-trip in *Sometimes A Great Notion.*

It is a book which seems to me not so much a second novel as a first novel written (or, perhaps, only published) second: a more literary, conventionally ambitious, and therefore *strained* effort—for all its occasional successes, somehow an error. *One Flew Over the Cuckoo's Nest* works better to the degree that it is dreamed or hallucinated rather than merely written—which is to say, to the degree that it, like its great prototype *The Leatherstocking Tales,* is Pop Art rather than *belles lettres*—the dream once dreamed in the woods, and now redreamed on pot and acid.

Its very sentimentality, good-guys bad-guys melodrama, occasional obviousness and thinness of texture, I find—like the analogous things in Cooper—not incidental flaws, but part of the essential method of its madness. There is a phrase which reflects on Kesey's own style quite early in the book, defining it aptly, though it pretends only to represent Chief Bromden's vision of the world around him: "Like a cartoon world, where the figures are flat and outlined in black, jerking through some kind of goofy story that might be real funny if it weren't for the cartoon figures being real guys. . . ."

Everywhere in Kesey, as a matter of fact, the influence of comics and, especially, comic books is clearly perceptible, in the mythology as well as in the style; for like those of many younger writers of the moment, the images and archetypal stories which underlie his fables are not the legends of Greece and Rome, not the fairy tales of Grimm, but the adventures of Captain Marvel and Captain Marvel, Jr., those new-style Supermen who, sometime just after World War II, took over the fantasy of the young. What Western elements persist in Kesey are, as it were, first translated back into comic-strip form, then turned once more into words on the conventional book page. One might, indeed, have imagined Kesey ending up as a comic book writer, but since the false second start of *Sometimes A Great Notion,* he has preferred to live his comic strip rather than write or even draw it.

The adventures of Psychedelic Superman as Kesey had dreamed and acted them, however—his negotiations with Hell's Angels, his being busted for the possession of marijuana, his consequent experiences in court and, as a refugee from the law, in Mexico—all this, like the yellow bus in which he used to move up and down the land taking an endless, formless movie, belongs to hearsay and journalism rather than to literary criticism, challenging conventional approaches to literature even as it challenges literature itself. But *One Flew Over the Cuckoo's Nest* survives the experiments and rejections which followed it; and looking back five years after its initial appearance, it seems clear that in it for the first time the New West was clearly defined: the West of Here and Now, rather than There and Then—the West of Madness.

The Westering impulse which Europe had begun by regarding as blasphemous (as, for instance, in Dante's description of Ulysses sailing through the Pillars of Hercules toward "the world without people"), it learned soon to think of as crazy, mocking Columbus and his dream of a passage to India, and condemning as further folly each further venture into a further West after the presence of America had been established (think, for example, of Cabeza de Vaca walking into the vast unknown and becoming, on his impossible adventure, a god to those savages whose world he penetrated).

It is only a step from thinking of the West as madness to regarding madness as the true West, but it took the long years between the end of the fifteenth century and the middle of the twentieth to learn to take that step. There is scarcely a New Western among those I have discussed which does not in some way flirt with the notion of madness as essential to the New World; but only in Leonard Cohen (though Thomas Berger comes close) and in Kesey is the final identification made, and in Kesey at last combined with the archetype of the love that binds the lonely white man to his Indian comrade—to his *mad* Indian comrade, perhaps even to the *madness* of his Indian comrade, as Kesey amends the old tale.

We have come to accept the notion that there is still a territory unconquered and uninhabited by palefaces, the bearers of "civilization," the cadres of imperialist reason; and we have been learning that into this territory certain psychotics, a handful of "schizophrenics," have moved on ahead of the rest of us—unrecognized Natty Bumppos or Huck Finns, interested not in claiming the New World for any Old God, King, or Country, but in becoming New Men, members of just such a New Race as D. H. Lawrence foresaw. (How fascinating, then, that R. D. Laing, leading exponent among contemporary psychiatrists of the theory that some schizophrenics have "broken through" rather than "broken down," should, despite the fact that he is an Englishman, have turned to our world and its discovery in search of an analogy; he suggests that Columbus's stumbling upon America and his first garbled accounts of it provide an illuminating parallel to the ventures of certain madmen into the regions of extended or altered consciousness, and to their confused version, once they are outside of it, of the strange realm in which they have been.)

Obviously, not everyone is now prepared, and few of us ever will be, to make a final and total commitment to the Newest West via psychosis; but a kind of tourism into insanity is already possible for those of us not yet ready or able to migrate permanently from the world of reason. We can take, as the New Westerns suggest, what is already popularly called—in the aptest of metaphors—a "trip," an excursion into the unknown with the aid of drugs. The West has seemed to us for a long time a place of recreation as well as of risk; and this is finally fair enough, for all the ironies implicit in turning a wilderness into a park. After all, the West remains always in some sense true to itself, as long as the Indian, no matter how subdued, penned off, or costumed for the tourist trade, survives—as long as we can confront there a creature radically different from the old self we seek to recreate in two weeks' vacation.

And while the West endures, the Western demands to be written—that form which represents a traditional and continuing dialogue between whatever old selves we transport out of whatever East, and the radically different other whom we confront in whatever West we attain. That other is the Indian still, as from the beginning, though only vestigially, nostalgically now; and also, with special novelty and poignancy, the insane.

If a myth of America is to exist in the future, it is incumbent on our writers, no matter how square and scared they may be in their deepest hearts, to conduct with the mad just such a dialogue as their predecessors learned long ago to conduct with the aboriginal dwellers in the actual Western Wilderness. It is easy to forget, but essential to remember, that the shadowy creatures living scarcely imaginable lives in the forests of Virginia once seemed as threatening to all that good Europeans believed as the acid-head or the borderline schizophrenic on the Lower East Side now seems to all that good Americans have come to believe in its place.

INDEX

Abraham, 69
Adam, 38, 40, 109
Adams, Henry, 81-2
Affecting History . . . of Frederic Manheim's Family, The, 93
Agatha, 54-5
Allen, Donald, 171
Ambassadors, The, 19
"America," 11
American, The, 20
American Dream, An, 157
American Magazine for Entertaining and Useful Knowledge, The, 103
Anderson, Sherwood, 145
Arthur, King, 30
Ashe, Geoffrey, 31
Atlantic Monthly, 81
At Play in the Fields of the Lord, 171-2
Augustine, St., 29, 38

Baldwin, James, 20
Ballad of Dingus Magee, The, 153, 160, 174
Bampico, 103, 108, 115, 118, 120
Barker, James Nelson, 64-5, 67
Barlowe, Joel, 94
Barth, John, 14, 15, 81, 150-2, 159, 161, 175
Baudelaire, Pierre Charles, 176
"Bear, The," 116-7, 142, 145, 179
Beautiful Losers, 155-7, 165, 176-7
Bellow, Saul, 60
"Benjamin Pantier," 59
Berger, Thomas, 14, 135, 160, 162, 163, 164, 183, 185
Bible, The, 31, 33, 37-8, 40, 101, 102, 107, 111, 114, 154
Big Sky, The, 137, 160
Birth of a Nation, The, 18, 139
Bleeker, Anna Eliza, 92, 95

Book of Mormon, 23
Bostonians, The, 20
Brendan-Brandan, St., 31-2, 33
Bridge, The, 55, 63, 84, 88-9
Brother to Dragons, 92, 128, 136
Brougham, John, 81
Brown, Brockden, 128
Bumppo, Natty, 12, 25, 51, 59, 60, 117-8, 121, 124, 140, 162, 167, 173, 182, 185
Burgess, Anthony, 175
Burke, Charles, 61
Burroughs, Edgar Rice, 93
Burroughs, William, 15, 175

Cabeza de Vaca, 185
Cabot Wright Begins, 177-8
Calamity Jane, 160
Caliban, 42-3, 45-9, 66
Cantos, 55
Capote, Truman, 14, 18
Captain Marvel, 184
Cat Ballou, 14, 23, 150
Chapters of Erie, 81
Chingachgook, 12, 28, 51, 117-8, 121, 126, 140, 162, 167, 182
Clansman, The, 18, 139
Clarissa, 68
Clark, Walter Van Tilburg, 142-3
Clark, William, 72-5, 128, 130, 131, 134-5, 156
Clockwork Orange, The, 175
Cohen, Leonard, 14, 155-7, 164, 165, 166, 175-7, 185
Coleridge, Samuel Taylor, 176
Columbus, Christopher, 22, 27, 31, 34, 36-40, 42, 85, 107, 120, 185, 186
Columbus, Ferdinand, 37, 38
Confidence Man, The, 81, 96, 124
Connecticut Yankee in King Arthur's Court, A, 21

Cooper, Gary, 136, 143, 147, 150, 159, 173
Cooper, James Fenimore, 20, 22, 23, 28, 51, 60, 75, 98, 117-8, 121-2, 123, 124, 126, 127, 128, 129, 130, 133-4, 138, 140, 141, 167, 184
Copland, Aaron, 88
Cortez, Hernando, 79
Cosmographie Introductio, 65
Crane, Hart, 55-6, 63-4, 84, 87-9, 104, 105, 165
Crawley, Alastair, 154
Creeley, Robert, 171
Crèvecoeur, St. John de, 111, 169
Critias, 32-3
"Curse on the Men in Washington, Pentagon, A," 86-7
Custer, George Armstrong, 76, 160
Custis, George Washington Parke, 64

Dante Alighieri, 21, 27, 33-6, 37, 38, 42, 43, 47, 120, 185
Day of the Locust, The, 144, 147-9, 150, 159
Deerslayer, The, 122
de las Casas, Bartolomé, 40, 41
De Quincy, Thomas, 176
Dixon, Thomas, Jr., 18, 139, 142
Donleavy, J. P., 11
Dorn, Ed, 13
Duston, Hannah, 51, 52, 90-1, 95, 97, 98-108, 115, 116, 118, 144, 180, 181, 182
Duston, Thomas, 99-100, 103-4, 105, 114

Earp, Wyatt, 160
Eastlake, William, 171, 175
Eliot, T. S., 21, 55, 122
Enoch Arden, 55
Ethan Frome, 17
Eve, 107, 109, 118
Events in Indian History, 102

Faerie Queene, The, 44
"Fathers and Sons," 144
Faulkner, William, 18, 57, 116, 136, 142, 143, 144, 145, 153, 179
Faust, Clarence, 121
"Fenimore Cooper's Literary Offenses," 122

"First Spade in the West, The," 135, 153, 159
Fisher, Vardis, 128
Fitzgerald, F. Scott, 21, 57
Flaubert, Gustave, 34, 81
Fleming, E. McClung, 65-6
Flynn, Thomas, 61
Fortune Cookie, The, 177
For Whom the Bell Tolls, 21, 144
France, Anatole, 151
Franklin, Benjamin, 57
Freud, Sigmund, 91
Frontier: American Literature and the American West, 129
Frost, Robert, 17, 26
Fu Manchū, Dr., 93
Fussell, Edwin, 129

Gable, Clark, 157
Geddes, Vergil, 64
Generall Historie, 70
Ginger Man, The, 11-12
Ginsberg, Allen, 11
Giovanni's Room, 20
Girty, Simon, 140, 169
God's Mercy Surmounting Man's Cruelty, as Exemplified in the Captivity and Surprising Deliverance of Elizabeth Hanson, 93
Gone With the Wind, 18
Gordon Pym, 98, 129-31, 162
Graham, Martha, 88
Grande Encyclopédie, 79
Grey, Zane, 121, 142
Griffith, D. W., 18, 139
Guthrie, A. B., 137

Hakluyt, Richard, 36
Hall, James, 124-6
Hanging Tree, The, 143
Harlowe, Jean, 147
Hawthorne, Nathaniel, 20, 51, 54-5, 90, 103-4, 105, 120, 122, 128
Hemingway, Ernest, 14, 21, 57, 143-6, 149, 150-1, 172-4
Henry, Alexander, 51, 90, 109-19, 124, 130, 162, 167, 182
Henry VIII, 45
Hercules, 34
Herlihy, James Leo, 14, 153-4, 159
Hesiod, 30
Hickok, Wild Bill, 160
High Noon, 139, 157

189

History of Greece, 44
History of Maria Kittle, The, 92, 93, 95
Holmes, Oliver Wendell, 54
Homer, 30, 82
Homeward Bound, 20
Howells, William Dean, 17
Huckleberry Finn, 19, 57, 60, 90-1, 120, 126-7, 161, 178, 181, 182, 185
Hudson, Henry (Hendrick), 59, 60

In Cold Blood, 14
"Indian Camp," 144
The Indian Princess, or La Belle Sauvage, 64
Inferno, 33, 35, 41, 120
Injun Joe, 178
Innocents Abroad, 21, 123
Invention of America, The, 36
Irving, Washington, 51, 53-61, 103
Ishmael, 60, 98, 120, 182
Isidore of Seville, 31, 36
Ivanhoe, 69, 138, 141

James, Henry, 17, 19-20, 21, 25, 122, 143
Jefferson, Joseph, III, 60-2, 63
Jefferson, Thomas, 73, 92, 128, 132, 133
Jemison, Mery, 95-6
Jim, 19, 28, 120, 126-7, 178, 183
Johnson, Dorothy, 143
Journal of Julius Rodman, 128, 131-6, 160
Journals of Lewis and Clark, The, 128, 133-5
Joyce, James, 11, 81

Kahn, Otto, 64, 88
Kavanaugh: A Tale, 20
Kenyon Review, 56, 67
Kerr, John, 61
Kesey, Ken, 14, 60, 153, 154-5, 164, 177, 178, 179-85

Ladd, Allan, 160
La Farge, Oliver, 170, 175
Laing, R. D., 185-6
Land to the West, 31
Last of the Mohicans, The, 118, 134
Laughing Boy, 170

Lawrence, D. H., 11, 22, 30, 31, 49, 57, 111, 145, 162, 163, 165-6, 167, 185
Layton, Irving, 157
Leatherstocking Tales, 98, 121, 122, 127, 138, 183
Leaves of Grass, 77
Leavis, F. R., 122
Leonardson, Samuel, 100
Leopard's Spots, The, 139, 142
"Letter to the Sovereigns," 37-8
Letters from an American Farmer, 169
Lewis, Meriwether, 72-4, 128, 130, 131-4, 136, 156
Lewis, Wyndham, 84-5
Light in August, 179
Lindsay, Vachel, 84, 86, 87
Little Big Man, 135, 160, 162-3, 183
Longfellow, Henry Wadsworth, 20, 21, 63, 64, 77-8
Lord of the Rings, The, 53, 175
Loudon, Archibald, 94-5
Love and Death in the American Novel, 7, 53
Love's Labour's Lost, 43
Lowell, Robert, 17

Macrobius, 36
Mad Bear, 12-13
Magic Mountain, 154
Magnalia Christi Americana, 90, 101
Magnani, Anna, 84
Mailer, Norman, 14, 157
Man Who Killed the Deer, The, 170
Mann, Thomas, 154
Manzoni, Alessandro, 122
Marble Faun, The, 20
Marina (Malintzin), 79-80, 156
Markson, David, 14, 153, 161, 164, 174
Marlowe, 176
Marvin, Lee, 150, 159
Mary, the Mother of Christ, 69
Masters, Edgar Lee, 59
Mather, Cotton, 51, 90, 92, 94, 100-2, 103-4, 105, 107, 116
Matthews, Harry, 175
Matthiessen, Peter, 14, 171, 175
Maugham, Somerset, 171
Maupassant, Guy de, 81
Mayflower, The, 17
McCarty, William, 67

McLuhan, Marshall, 49
Medea, 37
Melville, Herman, 28, 35, 54-5, 60, 81, 96, 98, 120, 122, 124, 125, 143
Merchant of Venice, The, 69, 70
Merrill, James, 96-7
Midnight Cowboy, 153-4, 159
Miller, Arthur, 157
Milton, John, 107
Minister's Wooing, The, 17
Misfits, The, 157-8
Mitchell, Margaret, 18
Mitchum, Robert, 143
Moby Dick, 98, 120, 129, 142
Monroe, Marilyn, 84, 156-8
Montaigne, Michel Eyquem de, 40-2, 43, 46, 47, 48, 52
Montezuma, 79
Moredock, Colonel John, 124-6
Morgan, 175
Morris, George P., 67-8
"Mother of Us All, The," 67

Navigatio Sancti Brendani, 33, 37
Neal, John, 128
New American Story, 171
Newton, Isaac, 114
Christopher Newman, 25
New World Planted, A, 68
Noah, 29, 31, 40
Nova Express, 175
"Now I Lay Me," 144

O'Connor, Flannery, 18
O'Gorman, Edmundo, 36
Oliver Twist, 57
One Flew Over the Cuckoo's Nest, 60, 178, 180-3, 184-5
"On the Cannibals," 40-2
"Our Mother Pocahontas," 86
Oxbow Incident, The, 142-3, 160

Pale-Face, 84
Pamela, 68, 70, 81, 156
Paris Review, 15
Paradise Lost, 107
Pathfinder, The, 122
Pausanias, 44
Peattie, Donald Culross, 74-5
Pericles, 49, 80
"Peter Klaus the Goatherd," 56
Pickwick Papers, The, 53
Pigafetta, 43

Plato, 32-3, 36, 82
Pocahontas, 50-1, 52, 64-72, 74-5, 78-83, 84-90, 95, 105, 107, 109-10, 111, 112, 118, 128, 131, 137, 145, 149, 150-3, 156-8, 161, 162, 165, 167
Pocahontas and the Elders, 64
Poe, Edgar Allan, 18, 98, 127-36, 160, 176
Polo, Marco, 22
"Portrait of an Artist with 26 Horses," 171
Pound, Ezra, 21, 34, 55
Powhatan, 69, 71, 90, 151-2, 156
Prairie, The, 22, 121
Pudd'nhead Wilson, 82, 178
Purdy, James, 177-8
Purgatorio, 35

Queequeg, 28, 98, 120, 182

Raleigh, Sir Walter, 176
Real Legends of New England, 102
"Red Leaves," 116
Rice, Thomas D., 61
Richardson, Samuel, 68, 70, 80, 81
Riders of the Purple Sage, 142, 157
"Rip Van Winkle," 51, 52, 53-62, 63, 64, 80, 87-8, 90, 104, 112, 118
"Rip Van Winkle's Lilac," 54
Robinson Crusoe, 53
Robinson, Edward Arlington, 17
Rolfe, John, 70, 71, 85, 86, 162, 167
Roman Spring of Mrs. Stone, The, 19
Rousseau, Jean Jacques, 41, 80, 94, 124
Rowlandson, Mary, 51
Russell, Charlie, 137

Sacajawea, 72-5, 78, 80, 131, 134, 137, 156
Sandburg, Carl, 84, 85-6
Scarlet Letter, The, 17, 120-1
Scott, Sir Walter, 69, 122, 138, 140
Sebastian, St., 89
Seneca, 37
Sepúlveda, Juan Ginés de, 40

191

Shakespeare, William, 40-1, 42-9, 51, 52, 69, 70, 80, 156
Shane, 143, 160
Ship of Fools, 150
Sitting Bull, 76
Smith, James, 111
Smith, Captain John, 50-1, 63, 67-72, 81-3, 85, 88, 90, 109, 111, 118, 128, 149, 150-2, 156, 159, 161, 162, 165, 167
Snyder, Gary, 86-7
Sometimes a Great Notion, 153, 154-5, 183-4
Song of Hiawatha, The, 77-8
Sot-Weed Factor, The, 81, 150-3, 161
Spenser, Edmund, 44
Spoon River Anthology, 59
Stowe, Harriet Beecher, 17
Strachey, William, 71, 85
Studies in Classic American Literature, 11, 111, 166
Sun Also Rises, The, 21, 145
Superman, 184

Tarzan, 93
Tekakwitha, Catherine, 79, 80, 99, 155-7, 165, 177
Tempest, The, 40-1, 42-9, 50
"Ten Little Indians," 144
Tender Is the Night, 21
Tennyson, Alfred, 55
Thoreau, Henry David, 17, 51, 90, 100, 104-8, 109-10, 112-6, 119, 120
Timaeus, 32-3
Titus Andronicus, 43
Tlooth, 175
Tolkien, J. R. R., 53, 175
Tom Sawyer, 90-1, 123, 126-7
Torrents of Spring, The, 143-4, 145-6, 150, 172
Track of the Cat, The, 142-3
True Relation of Virginia, A, 81, 151
Twain, Mark, 19, 21, 28, 60, 81-3, 84, 122-7, 177, 178

Ulysses, 33-5, 36, 55, 120, 184
Uncle Tom's Cabin, 17

"Vanishing Red, The," 26
Virginian, The, 138-41, 157
Voltaire, 151
Voyage of Bran, 31-2

Waiting for the End, 7
"Wakefield," 55
Walden, 17
Waldseemuller, Martin, 65
Warhol, Andy, 84
Warren, Robert Penn, 92, 128, 136, 137
Waste Land, The, 55
Watchful Gods, The, 142
Waters, Frank, 170-1, 175
Watts, Alan, 154
Wawatam, 51, 52, 60, 109-10, 112-6, 118-9, 120, 126, 138, 162, 167, 182
Wayne, John, 147
Week on the Concord and Merrimack Rivers, A, 17, 104-8
West, Nathanael, 144, 147-9, 150, 158
Wharton, Edith, 17
What Are We Doing in Vietnam? 14
Whitman, Walt, 27, 77, 84, 85, 87
Williams, Tennessee, 19, 84
Wilson, Edmund, 13
Wimer, James, 102
Wister, Owen, 138-9
"Witch of Coos, The," 17
Wodehouse, P. G., 53
Wonder Book, The, 54
Wyandotté, 127

York, 73, 134-6, 160
Young, Philip, 56, 67, 69

Zola, Emile, 81